ESSAYS ON FATHERHOOD

Anecdotes of a Father's Journey toward Wisdom

JAMES SHERMAN

CLAY BRIDGES
PRESS

Essays on Fatherhood
Anecdotes of a Father's Journey toward Wisdom

Copyright © 2020 by James Sherman

Published by Clay Bridges in Houston, TX
www. ClayBridgesPress. com

Some names have been changed for privacy.

Scripture quotations are taken from the ESV® Bible (The Holy Bible, English Standard Version®), copyright © 2001 by Crossway, a publishing ministry of Good News Publishers. Used by permission. All rights reserved.

ISBN: 978-1-7352217-2-4
eISBN: 978-1-7352217-6-2

Special Sales: Most Clay Bridges titles are available in special quantity discounts. Custom imprinting or excerpting can also be done to fit special needs. Contact Clay Bridges at Info@ClayBridgesPress.com.

TABLE OF CONTENTS

TIMELINE

1972 Jim and Linda marry; Jim begins medical school at University of South Florida

1974 Scott is born

1976 Chris is born

1981 Jim completes training as a pediatric pulmonologist, takes his first job at the University of South Florida

1982 Timothy (Timo) is born

1984 Kenneth is born

1986 Kristin is born

1988 Karin is born, dies six months later; family relocates to Vermont

1990 Rachel is born

1991 Dorothy is born

1994 Ben is born; family relocates to Florida; Jim works at University of Florida Department of Pediatrics

1999 Family purchases Maple Ridge, moves trailer onto property

2001 Jim is diagnosed with cancer

2004 Family relocates to Roanoke; Jim works for Carilion Medical System

2005 Foundation poured at Maple Ridge

2006 Timber frame is erected; Maple Ridge is under construction

2017 Jim retires and works full-time on Maple Ridge

2019 Maple Ridge is completed

FOREWORD

Essays on Fatherhood is a book of stories and reflections about one man's journey to try to become the best father he can be. As such, it is a great read for all kinds of fathers—fathers-to-be, new fathers in the throes of raising small children, fathers who face the challenges of adolescents, and older fathers with grown children who now reflect on their roles as parents. It's also a great read for those folks you know who will never become a father but probably had one along the way (e. g. , mothers).

Each of Sherman's stories about childrearing is written from a personal perspective that only a father of nine unique children can bring. New fathers may have their eyes opened or be surprised. Older or more seasoned fathers may smile, be moved, or be reminded. Amusing, tender, complicated, and sometimes unsettling stories become parables for parents. After reading *Essays on Fatherhood* and whether or not you agree with his insights, you will likely think deeply about the kind of relationships you want to have with your children.

I have known the author, Jim Sherman, for more than 40 years. We first met as medical students, then worked as pediatric interns and residents in the same hospital, and finally were practicing physicians and teachers together in the same academic Department of Pediatrics. Jim is no ordinary doctor; he is no ordinary anything. He loves being a pediatrician, and he loves teaching. He's extraordinarily good at both. And he lives with a fierce commitment to excellence and professionalism in all that he does. But as much as he loves being a doctor and a teacher, they pale compared to his love for his family.

Essays on Fatherhood is about what a deeply spiritual and principled man has learned dealing with the big issues parents face in raising children today. You will learn that the fun, fears, bewilderments, and joys you experience in childrearing are a whole lot more common than you may think. You will also learn how we fathers can grow in wisdom and maturity through introspection, reflection, spiritual study, and a willingness to honestly and vulnerably confront our own strengths, faults, weaknesses, and preconceived ideas about raising children. This is a book of celebration. You'll find it a gift to you and your children.

—Douglas Barrett, MD

INTRODUCTION

Novelist and essayist George Santayana once wrote in *The Life of Reason* (1905), "Those who cannot remember the past are condemned to repeat it." This idea is true for nations, for governments, and for individuals. It is true for big moments in history and for small moments in our day-to-day lives. History can be something successful or something that failed. *Essays on Fatherhood* is about my personal history—including my failures—and the lessons I learned. Because I have an abundance of confidence and a deficit of caution, I have bumbled my way into plenty of failures (or mistakes or sins). When I worked as an attendant at a full-service gas station, my boss described me to a company manager like this: "Sherman makes about every mistake in the book, but he only makes that mistake once." While I appreciate that comment, it is not correct. Unfortunately, I have made some mistakes over and over before I finally recognized them as a problem, and sometimes a spectacular, painful problem. I think God works that way—if you don't get it the first time, the ante gets upped. Fortunately, He didn't give up on me, and eventually I recognized my failure to be holy, as God is holy. My children have encouraged me that my fatherhood was not just a series of mistakes but has largely been a success. They will add to these essays to highlight the aspects they consider most important.

I wrote these essays because my children encouraged me to do so. They love these stories and think the tales only get better with time. Although they don't always remember the stories exactly as I do, they all agree that they are true and not made up to make a point. But why am I writing this book now when life's lessons are still coming? There are several reasons. I have finally finished building Maple Ridge, our home (there are essays about this house in the pages that follow). Linda, my wife, also says I need another project or our marriage is in jeopardy (I think she is exaggerating since my suggestions to her about how to run the house are always very reasonable). Finally, I am 73, and my physician tells me my chance of a stroke or major cardiovascular event in the next five years is about 20 percent. So if I am going to do this, it seems the time is now.

These essays are not sequential; they are loosely grouped by subject matter. Some were written as many as 25 years ago and others within the last year. My hope is that reading about my journey will not only entertain you but give you something to take away. I hope you might learn from my mistakes and be encouraged that you can do better. I could not write so publicly about my sins and errors if I had less assurance that Christ paid for my sins—those I committed up to the time I accepted Him and those I have committed since then.

FATHERS DURING DELIVERY

My last job during my medical career was as a newborn nursery doctor. I made rounds throughout the hospital nursery in the mornings, and my routine was to introduce myself, examine the newborn, discuss findings and plans, and deal with any problems. My interactions were with mothers. Dads, if present, would sit or lie on the couch and usually not involve themselves in the process. Having been on the couch myself on a number of occasions, I have some sympathy for their plight.

Men are fairly peripheral to the process of birth. They typically have some sense of guilt during the painful time of labor. They acknowledge that they are the cause of this pregnancy, but the consequences of labor are all hers to bear. Men play a supportive role. They encourage, mop the sweat from the brow of the laboring mother, and suffer along with her. They pray, hope, and love. After the delivery, the baby is given to the mother for bonding and perhaps to nurse. Dad can only gaze at this scene of maternal bliss and be grateful the delivery is finally over. Nurses, doctors, and visitors shower congratulations and praise on the mother for her wonderful accomplishment. Any congratulations to Dad are less enthusiastic (unless they come from his mother). The labor suite and the nursery are female-dominated in their staffing and their orientation. Dads sense their presence is tolerated but not particularly helpful.

On occasion, when I sensed the opening, I would spend some extra time in the room focused on the father.

"So, Dad, how did you do during the delivery?"

"I think I did pretty well. I didn't faint."

"Were you supportive and there for your wife?"

"Yeah, I think so." (Looks to wife for her nod of agreement that he did well in his role, minor though it might have been.)

"Great! Has anyone congratulated you for the important role you played in the delivery?"

"Well, they said congratulations, but I think that was more for just having had a child."

"On a number of occasions, during the birth of one of my children or at an office visit later on, I have felt like a piece of furniture," I would say. "As a man who has been through what you have just been through, let me say that I recognize your vital and important contributions to your family and heartily congratulate you on your accomplishments." (Mother is smiling, perhaps in disbelief at this conversation, but I am concentrating on Dad. He seems pleased to have been recognized.) "If you are feeling a little neglected, I am here for you. Need a hug?"

"Nah, I'm good."

I turn back to Mom to discuss further business. After some more interaction, now with both the mother and father since I have invited him into the conversation, I begin to conclude the visit. On a couple of occasions, I would then hear, "Dr. Sherman, I think I would like the hug." Mom was usually openly laughing by this time, but Dad and I felt pretty good about things. It's nice to be appreciated even if you know you weren't all that important to the process.

FAMILY AND JOB BALANCE

"Elaine, you don't look very happy. What's going on?" One of our chief residents, a bright, talented doctor, looked like she was carrying a heavy load.

"Just some trouble at home," she replied. But what she didn't say was "it's nothing serious," and her body language wasn't shutting me out. I felt she wanted to tell me more.

"Why don't we talk about it?" I suggested.

Elaine was in her third year of residency. I had worked closely with her and thought she had a career in academic medicine if she wanted it. She had been talking about completing either an infectious disease or pulmonary fellowship at a prestigious institution. As we talked, it became evident that her husband, a nuclear engineer, had made a number of moves and job changes to accommodate her training needs and was balking at another one. It had come down to this: He didn't want to go where she wanted to go. Would she leave her husband, or would she give up her dream? She didn't want either option.

I suggested that perhaps Elaine's husband felt he was less important to her than her job and wasn't happy with second place. We talked through it. Eventually, she said, "You are lucky. Men don't have these kinds of problems. In your family, you never have to choose between family and career."

"You're correct that I've never had to make that kind of decision," I acknowledged. "But someday I might have to. My job is important, but not more important than my relationship with God and not more important than my duties as a father and husband. If I ever find them in conflict, the job is the one that has to change." She didn't argue further, but I'm not sure she believed me.

The next day I saw Elaine again. She looked peaceful. "I talked with Rob last night," she said. "When I told him that I understood my actions had been saying the career was more important than he was, he was surprised. He suddenly stopped looking mad and looked touched. When I told him I would follow his lead and make do with whatever opportunities I could find in the location that was best for him, he was astonished. He even started to cry. We've worked out a move that will work out for both of us—not the best for him or for me, but best for us as a couple. Thank you for helping. I'm very happy."

A few years later during the 25-minute drive from the hospital to my office, I was listening to *Focus on the Family*, the James Dobson radio show. The discussion that day was about workaholics, and there was a listing of characteristics workaholics often have. I fit nearly all of them, and for good reason. The men I admired—men who had trained me, men who had set a standard of excellence in patient care, in scholarly activity, and in service to their community— had these characteristics, too. I felt some sense of pride, or at least accomplishment, that I had what it took to be successful in the same sense as they were. Plus, I felt my family was doing okay. I seldom ate dinner with them, but I did spend time with them in the morning and went with them to church. I provided for them. I had good kids, and Linda wasn't complaining (at least she had no reasonable complaints, although sometimes there were unreasonable ones). The family was okay, and I was on track to accomplish many of my professional goals. I was doing fine.

Two years later, my university informed me that I was about to lose the vacation time I had stored up, and any further time I earned would not be saved. I took a month off and went with my family to Vermont to visit friends. I had trained with Chas, the husband of the family, and had been present at the delivery of his first son. Chas often asked me if I wanted to join his practice, but I had no desire to go into the community practice of pediatrics. We stayed with the family for a week and had an absolutely eye-opening experience. Chas was (and is) a very good doctor, yet he manages to craft his life so it revolves around his family. They had draft and riding horses, they had property in a rural area, they tapped maple trees, and they did "stuff," finding great pleasure in the time they spent together. Chas had one weekday off each week and *never* did medical stuff on that day. The day was for family time. His life and his focus were so different from mine that I was embarrassed, challenged, and knocked off my foundation. While my children weren't failing, they were clearly not thriving in the presence of an involved and loving father. Linda had been doing the jobs of both father and mother and doing well at them, but one parent cannot replace the involvement of two.

To her credit, Linda never looked me in the eye and said, "Chas is a lot better father and husband than you are," though she would have been justified in doing so. I think, in fact, that she was as taken off guard as I was. Within the peer group we had at the University of South Florida (USF), the adjustments we had made to my workaholic nature were pretty general. Linda didn't need to say anything, however, as I could see it for myself.

A couple of months after returning to work, I got a call from the associate chairman asking me to take on a significant task that would require time and effort. He had good reason to call me since I was the right person for this job, and I agreed to take it on. He then asked me what he could do for me, thinking, I suspect, that I would suggest a significant monetary bonus at year's end. I responded, "What I really want is more time with my family." There was silence for quite a while at the other end of the phone.

"I can't give you that," he replied softly.

"I don't need anything else," I said. The next time Chas called to offer me a position, I told him I would seriously consider it.

Leaving academic medicine was not an easy decision for me. My family wasn't failing by any usual standard. Taking this job would mean giving up career goals I had set, goals I was on track to reach. I knew that many would not understand such a decision. Did God really want me to give up so much? Why would He have me waste all that training? Didn't He want me to serve him in a prestigious setting and position? Wouldn't I be able to serve Him better at a university than in a small community? As I lay in bed one night and wrestled with these thoughts, I suddenly recalled a verse: "As for what was sown among thorns, this is the one who hears the word, but the cares of the world and the deceitfulness of riches choke the word, and it proves unfruitful (Matt. 13:22). After that, the way was clear. I resigned from USF, and in September of that year, we moved to join a pediatric practice in northern Vermont.

Years later, I heard my son Scott talking to a group about that move. With tears in his eyes and a catch in his voice, he said, "Dad loved us enough that he gave up a career for us." It was not until that moment that I really knew how important that move was to him. The move certainly made a big difference in the lives of my children, but even more certain was the change it made in the life of the one who needed it most—me. Had I not made that decision when it was presented so clearly to me, I would have been valuing my career as more important than either God or family, and the long-term consequences of that kind of decision are frightening.

Six years later, I received a letter from a search committee at the University of Florida informing me they were looking for a division chief in the Pediatric Pulmonary Division. Was I interested? For a while after our move to Vermont, I had been contacted by people in academic medicine offering me opportunities to return, but I dropped off the map after a couple of years and no longer got those inquiries. I took the letter home to show it to Linda and the kids at dinner. "Look, someone still knows I am alive," I said, and put the letter aside, thinking no more of it. The next day when I got home, Linda said, "We need to talk." She and the older boys had discussed it and thought I should investigate the opportunity. "Why?" I asked in surprise. "Don't you remember how it used to be? Surely, you don't want to return to that kind of life."

"Your family has different needs now," she pointed out. "Scott and Chris are about ready for college, and it is certainly not clear how we are going to be able to help them financially with that. And we think you may have matured enough that you can make better decisions and withstand the pressure." It was nice to know she and my sons thought I had matured.

Over the next year, I struggled with the decision to take the job at the University of Florida. This time, however, God let me know He didn't care if I went or stayed because He knew where my heart was and would bless whatever decision I made. We took the job (not I—it was a family decision), and, in retrospect, it worked out very well. The 10 years I spent at the University of Florida were the high point of my medical career. I loved it. I worked hard. I was successful. I was certainly made to feel like an important and valued part of the department, and I know I made a difference there. Most importantly, I was able to do it and still keep my priorities straight (at least I think I did).

Years later, I was asked to give the White Coat Address to the first-year medical students at Virginia Tech Carilion School of Medicine where I was a professor of pediatrics. This address is given in conjunction with issuing them their white coats, whereupon they accept the responsibilities of the profession. I was asked to give the address because the prior students had suggested to the dean of student affairs that I had something meaningful to share. I told the students and their families the story of my own family, emphasizing that dedication to the profession was key to becoming a good doctor, but you could not abandon your family in the process. I won't repeat all the details of that address, but I certainly could not have given it if I had not listened to God and the inner voice when they spoke to me. I never achieved what I might have if I had ignored them and stayed in academic medicine, but I never would have been the father and husband I became had I not left. I am convinced I made the right choice.

9

MAKING IT COUNT TWICE

Early in my academic career, I learned about the principle of making it count twice. Let me explain. We are sometimes faced with a project that will take some time and effort to successfully complete. It is often something that might not be first on our priority list, and it will take time away from other tasks. Academic life for physicians is often a combination of patient care, teaching, community service, and expanding our professional knowledge. The latter might not hold a prominent place in our work assignments, but it is critical in advancing our careers. The most common metric to measure the expansion of our knowledge is to publish articles in professional journals. If we can make the required project also work in another area (i.e., teaching, service, or publication), then it has worked twice. It probably means the initial work needs more time and effort, but it will take less time than two separate projects.

Faced with a very busy work life and a growing family, I made this principle work for me in fatherhood. In a later essay on jogging, I describe how I went from jogging alone because it met my personal need to jogging with all my children to meet the needs of our family time. Although about half of them did not like the activity, I felt their personal need for a healthy lifestyle and our shared need for productive time together were worth pushing the issue. Music is the subject of another essay, and for this shared time I got little push back. We all loved it. Building Maple Ridge, making maple syrup, learning animal husbandry, and cooking together are more projects we shared. They were all things that had value in themselves but were more valuable because they were meaningful in building relationships.

I have had friends remark that they find it significant that my children not only participated in these projects but also enjoyed and looked forward to family time. My friends have commented that they would be unable to take their children away from their social structures and devices for two weeks to build something with their family members. We never had that problem. Because my children grew up with family time, because we made sure they enjoyed the process, because we took pictures and made picture albums highlighting their contributions, and because we never made completion of a project more important than the enjoyment of hard work together with people we love, our children valued these projects. Scott, our firstborn, schedules time off from work to take his family on missions-related building projects. (He is smarter than I was since he makes it work three times: his family works together, learns construction skills, and is a blessing to those in need.) The other value I now see is that my children all have a well-developed work ethic. Our projects all involved work, and the product of that work had to be very good. We got there together, we were mutually supportive, and we enjoyed the process. Work became something good, not something to be avoided. Even if some aspect of it was not pleasant, the overall goal was seen as worth the effort.

While I have described some of the activities we made work twice, there were other activities I avoided, mostly because they would have been solitary activities. If I couldn't figure out a way to involve large segments of the family, I just didn't do the activity. I do not regret what I lost by this decision. My two oldest sons are 45 and 43 at this writing. I spent about 20 years raising them and have had more time than that valuing them as adult friends I admire. Fatherhood is an effort well worth doing well.

RAISING ANIMALS

"Everyone gets to choose," I announced. "When we move to Vermont, we'll live in the country and have enough property to have a bunch of animals. Each one of you can choose what animal to have." At that time, we had our first four boys and Kristin, who wanted bunnies. Scott wanted a horse. Kenneth chose dogs. Chris didn't really want anything but figured cats would be easy. Timo thought a horse was a really good idea but was pretty flexible. Linda wanted a milk cow. I wanted bees.

I grew up in a family without pets because my father was allergic. Linda had grown up with dogs, but neither of us had any significant experience with farm animals. The land we bought in Vermont was not set up as a farm, but there was a large woodshed we could convert into a small barn, and we could use electric fencing to keep the animals in our pastures. We were not experienced enough, however, to understand the challenges of keeping the animals where they belonged.

At one point after we had begun our small farm, Linda suggested naming our Vermont homestead Runaway Acres. Newly acquired pigs got out, and we found only one. While I was pulling some wood to the house, our horse Dick got away from me and bolted down the road, pulling the logs behind him. I got the car and dropped Scott off on the road ahead of him, about a quarter mile from the house. Dick had slowed down by the time we got there, and Scott was able to drive him back. Years later, our neighbors down the road were still chuckling about seeing our horse that day.

The most memorable escape happened one day when a farmer friend delivered Misty to us. Misty was a five-month-old Belgian mare and was Scott's project. The farmer also owned a turkey that had the run of his dairy farm and was a pet, but since the state inspectors didn't want the turkey in the dairy barn for sanitary reasons, it had to go. The farmer figured I could take the turkey, too, so he brought it to us along with Misty. When they arrived, Scott unloaded Misty, and we carefully introduced her to the other horses (we had Dick and a couple of boarders at the time). After chasing Misty around a little to establish a pecking order, the horses accepted her.

We were standing around talking and enjoying the weather while watching the horses in their pasture. The turkey had been strutting around pecking, preening, and doing turkey things. When she decided to visit the horses, we didn't think anything of it. She sauntered under the electric fence into the pasture, spread her wings, and gobbled a greeting to the herd of horses. Dick had never seen a turkey and reacted as though it were a devil from the darkest part of hell. He took off, snapped the electric fence like it was nothing, and bolted down the road. The rest of the horses sprinted after him, although I can't remember if Misty spooked, since she knew the turkey. Scott and I were a well-oiled team at this point—we ran for the truck, and I took off with Scott in the back. He jumped onto the neck of one of the boarders, got her under control, and led her back, the other boarder following soon after. Dick, having outrun the devil, was trotting calmly and easy for me to catch. Back we went.

We had lots of adventures with Dick. One day, Timo, who was about six at the time, was leading Dick from the barn out to the pasture. He got to the pasture gate, unclipped the lead, and released Dick. Glad to be out of the barn and full of energy, Dick took off around the pasture in a full gallop. Normally, I was thrilled to see him gallop; I could feel the earth shake with the weight of his pace, and it was a majestic sight. This particular time, though, I just felt panic. Before Dick left the barn, I had put Kristin (age two) on his back, made sure she had a grasp of his mane, and expected Timo to help her down. I can't remember if I actually told him Kristin was there, but in any case, by the time he got to the pasture, getting her down was not on his mind. Kristin lasted about three gallops, showing more and more air between her and Dick's back with each stride until she was airborne. As I sprinted to the pasture, I was worried she would fall under his feet, but by the time she hit the ground he was a good 20 feet away. She landed on her back in some soft Vermont spring mud and was fine. However, it took me a little longer to recover. Thank you, God, for protecting my children from their father's stupidity.

We heated our house with wood, so cutting, splitting, and getting the wood to the house was a significant task. One winter, Dick seemed very reluctant to go down the hill into the woods, and I had wood I needed to bring up. (I subsequently learned that it was too icy, and he was afraid of slipping. We later shod him with shoes fitted with spikes, called frogs, and it was never a problem again. I just didn't know.) Dick and I had a series of discussions about it, and I insisted that he go; eventually, I forced him. We had multiple trips to make, so this happened over and over. I was getting pretty frustrated, and I'm sure he wasn't happy, either. While dragging a load up through the pasture to the house, I slipped and fell. The gate was open, and I was afraid Dick would go off down the road again, so I held on to the reins, sliding through the icy pasture. The reins were long enough, so I was behind him, but I was still pretty close to his hooves, and I tried to swivel my body around so my head wouldn't get kicked. In the pasture, there were frozen clumps of horse manure, snow mixed with mud, and frozen ruts in the ground. Fortunately, Dick headed toward a corner of the fenced pasture and stopped. I regained control, and we finished the task. Later, I mentioned the episode to Linda. "I saw the whole thing from the window," she told me. "It was scary."

"It sure was," I acknowledged. "I was worried I was going to get kicked in the head or tear myself up on one of those frozen manure piles."

"Oh, I wasn't worried about you," Linda assured me. "I was worried you would get mad and hurt Dick."

I guess I didn't mind that she worried about Dick's welfare. It just seemed I should be worth a little worry, too.

One time, a family we knew from Florida visited us. While we were walking in the woods, Scott and Jordan, their oldest son, hitched Dick to the wagon for a ride. Coming toward us, Scott accidentally dropped the reins, and Dick started trotting. Scott knew he had to get the reins, so he jumped out, ran up, and caught Dick. Jordan, seeing Scott jump out, figured that was the best thing to do, so he did, too, and broke his arm in the fall. He was on his way to a golf scholarship at the University of Florida. I figured I was surely going to be sued, but his parents took it all in stride, and Jordan healed well.

We bought a second Belgian and had a team, Dick and Bud. We hauled logs for heat and for lumber; we hauled a gathering tank for sugaring; we went for wagon and sleigh rides for pleasure; we hauled hay. Their manure fertilized the garden. I learned to trim hooves and worm horses. I learned about rotational grazing. I don't know that I have ever been as exhilarated as I was when we went flying over a snow-covered field in a sleigh drawn by two powerful horses, snow flying from their hooves, bells jingling, and the children laughing. We loved having the horses and appreciated their strength, gentleness, and willingness to work. Those horses taught us many lessons.

The same farmer who sold us Misty eventually had to auction off his herd of cows. We wanted a family dairy cow, and he suggested we buy Polly, a 12-year-old Guernsey. Most commercial dairy cows last only about seven years before their feed costs more than their production. Polly was near that for a commercial cow and would have been bought by someone who would slaughter her, but the farmer knew she would be great for us. She was very gentle and let anyone milk her, and she gave us wonderful milk, about three to four gallons a day. Although that might sound like a lot, Holsteins can produce up to 10 gallons per day. Polly let goats and strange calves nurse on her. She raised a number of calves we bought for slaughter; we milked her once a day and let the calves stay on her the rest of the day. It worked well. When we left Vermont, Polly was still going strong, and we sold her to a man who also wanted a traditional family milk cow.

One of my patients gave me a goat. When I took it home, Linda asked, "What are we going to do with that?" A reasonable question. This particular goat was a pet, had lots of bad habits, and was a pest. It was also in desperate need of a hoof trim, but we had no idea how to do that. Linda asked around and heard of some people nearby who raised goats, so we made an appointment to visit them. They talked with us about goats, we drank some goat milk, we tried some homemade goat cheese, and we went home with new friends and more goats. Since no one had chosen goats when we moved there, an assignment had to be made. Chris became the goatherd and tolerated this with reasonable grace until Timo was old enough. What Chris tolerated, Timo later enjoyed, and he developed a gentle approach to his goats that amazed me. They became his pets, and he cried when his special ones had to be slaughtered. He got over it rapidly, though, and chevon (goat meat) remains one of his favorites.

We raised pigs, chickens, sheep, goats, rabbits, a turkey, two ducks, horses, cows, and about a thousand cats. We never did do bees. The children grew up eating animals they had raised and considered it normal. The only animals I had intended to eat but never did were the rabbits. There wasn't that much meat on them, and Kristin might never have forgiven me.

Our dogs—Ginger and Jill—were sisters. We got them when they were three or four years old. They had been used to ranging the country around their house. Their owners both worked and the family's children were grown, so they wanted the dogs to have children to play with. They were wonderful, beautiful dogs, about 7/8 Gordon Setter, a deep red in color, and they loved playing outdoors. Kenneth took care of them and did a great job. He almost lived in the basement with the dogs because I wouldn't let them in the rest of the house. In fact, many nights he slept with them rather than in his bed. The dogs especially loved it when we went cross-country skiing, and they raced along with us for hours. When we left Vermont, they went back to their original owners. By that time, they had slowed down some and were ready, I think, for a more sedate existence. They were the first dogs I ever liked.

Every morning when I left for work, the children went outside to care for their animals. Feeding, milking, cleaning the barn, and otherwise taking care of their animals had to be done seven days a week before they had breakfast or started school, work, or play. If there was any one thing I did to instill a solid work ethic in my children, it was giving them animals that depended on them. Every one of them did a very good job taking care of their charges, and some of them developed a deep affection for their animals, spending much more time with them than was required. When we moved back to Florida, we had a few animals, and one of the first things we did was fence in a 10-acre pasture and build a pole barn. Dick and Misty came to Florida with us, but Misty colicked and died in November the first year we were there, a very sad event for all of us. Somehow, the setting, the time of our life, and the other things going on around us kept us from really taking animal husbandry to Florida with us. Now that I'm retired, I have the time to have animals but have decided not to do so. They require daily care, and I want to be able to travel. We do have a dog, but she is easy to care for. One grandchild reminds me that I promised to buy her a horse. I have assured her I will do so as soon as her father tells me he is ready to have it at his house.

CHILDREN

We started having children without much thought about it. Linda became pregnant during our second year of marriage, and Scott was born during my second year of medical school. The pregnancy was uncomplicated, but the delivery was difficult. My uncle was chairman of the OB-GYN Department at the University of South Florida and was covering for Linda's obstetrician who was out of town. He did the delivery. Linda labored long and hard. Instead of coming through the birth canal headfirst looking down, Scott came looking up. You don't fit out as well that way, so the labor and pushing went on and on. When he was finally born, his head was shaped like a banana, he was little (5 pounds, 13 ounces), and he wasn't particularly attractive. One of the pediatric faculty, a neonatologist and friend of mine, commented, "If I ever saw a kid who should have been born by C-section, that is it."

All of Linda's deliveries were difficult and long, but none were as hard as her first, even though the children got bigger. By the time Linda had Benjamin, her uterus was pretty tired, and it didn't help much that he weighed 11 pounds. The obstetrician had to use forceps to pull him out. Forceps are really pretty interesting things. If the mother's bones and tissue would just get out of the way, the child would slide out pretty well. Babies are slimy, made to fit out, and the uterus is doing its best to get rid of them. The forceps fit around the head but don't squeeze it. As the obstetrician pulls the forceps out, they dilate and push away the tissues and bones, making a pathway for the child to follow. Depending on the degree of obstruction, that can be an easy or a difficult job. In Linda's case, it was hard, very hard.

She had two nurses grunting as they held her up on the delivery table. The obstetrician had his feet braced against the bottom of the table and was pulling so hard that his butt was off the stool. I had my head in the corner of the room, not wanting to look. Fortunately, both Linda and Ben were fine. Linda, as was usual for her, was delighted to hold her newborn and immediately forgot that there had been any difficulty. It took me somewhat longer to get over it.

We had been all over the place on the issue of controlling pregnancy. After Scott and Chris, we decided that two was a nice number and we could be done. Timo was a surprise, conceived despite our efforts, and the pregnancy was not particularly welcome. Linda had a lot of nausea throughout the pregnancy, and her obstetrician confided in me that it was likely the nausea was partly because she didn't want to be pregnant. She didn't get out of bed for much of that pregnancy, something she could do because Scott and Chris were in public school. Shortly after Timothy was born, we attended a seminar that taught that committed Christians should allow God to control their procreation. It seemed like a good idea to us, and children followed rapidly. My mother and father were somewhat aghast and concerned at the financial burden and health risks for Linda. Her mother and father were fine with it; they had attended the same seminar.

Over time, I began to have the idea that God gave me a brain and had put me in a position of spiritual and physical leadership in the family. It seemed that if I limited children from a selfish reason, it was my motive that failed to honor God. If I limited further children because I was concerned for my wife's health or our ability to continue to care for them, that was a different story. In any case, we would never have countenanced an abortion or abortive means of contraception but decided that other methods were appropriate if done with the correct motive. After nine live births, we decided it was enough.

The first four were boys. A couple of years after Kenneth was born, I was driving to work and suddenly just knew Linda was pregnant and that we were having a girl. I called her as soon as I got to work. "Guess what!" I exclaimed. "God just told me you are pregnant, and it's a girl." She started crying, and I was surprised because I thought she would be as excited as I was.

She explained, "Last night, I realized I was late and thought I might be pregnant. I thought you would be upset and told God that He would have to tell you. I didn't want to." She didn't know it was a girl, so at least I had something new to tell her. She had hoped for a girl so she could have someone to shop with.

I told everyone I knew that God had revealed to me that Linda was pregnant and that it was a girl—everyone at church, everyone at work, everyone I knew. We talked about girl names, we bought girl clothes. We never considered it would be a boy. Why should we? God had told me it was a girl. It wasn't until the day of the delivery that it suddenly occurred to me that I might possibly have misunderstood. I wasn't so worried about my reputation; everyone probably thought I was a little off anyway. I was worried about God's reputation, especially among the non-Christians I knew. But Kristin came out a girl, just as predicted.

So after the four boys came four girls. Karin followed Kristin, and in the delivery room, she seemed awfully blue. I listened carefully for a murmur but heard none. She cried and then settled down and initially seemed okay. It was when I took her to the sink to wash her off that I became aware that her neck skin folds were not normal. I finished washing her and looked at her again. She had the features of a child with trisomy 21, Down syndrome. I went to the NICU (neonatal intensive care unit) and asked one of my colleagues to look at my newborn. When he did, he confirmed my suspicions. With a heavy heart, I went to see Linda, sitting on the bed and telling her that Karin had Down syndrome and likely had bad heart disease. It was an emotional moment. Delivering a baby is an emotional high, exciting and miraculous. To follow that with the discovery that our child had a serious problem was somewhat shattering. Six months later, Karin required surgery for her severe cardiac problem, a surgery she did not survive.

God subsequently gave Linda the assurance he would send a "lamb" to us, not to replace Karin but to love. Rachel was that lamb. Dorothy followed, and then Ben. Our children are precious to us, each a gift from God. Eight children can be a lot sometimes, but I would not give up any of them. I was a better father after Scott and Chris tolerated my mistakes and taught me better ways. I became less rigid, more demonstrative, more attuned to the needs of my children. I learned by reflecting on my mistakes. I lost my temper less often. I didn't have to think as much about how to respond to them; I knew from previous experience. I'm not sure I was as good of a father to Ben as I was to some of the middle children (I was older, had less energy, more things were distracting me), but I am sure I was better than I was with Scott and Chris. When I was talking to Scott one time about some of the lessons I had learned from him, he commented, "Dad, you'd better stick around for a long time. I am going to need lots of that wisdom." I hope I do. It was hard to acquire it, and it would be nice to see it benefit my grandchildren. Eight *is* a lot, but it is the perfect number because it is what God wanted us to have. Nine was perfect, too. We look forward to time with Karin, healed in God's perfect wisdom, in our future.

At the time of this writing, we have 19 grandchildren. Our children's families vary in size from two to seven. Three of my children have no kids but likely will add to that total. Although all our children say they loved the experience of having a large family, not all of them are interested in replicating it. Some have gently approached me about how I might feel about their decisions to limit the size. I have assured them I have no thoughts or feelings about that decision; it is between them, their spouse, and God. "Like arrows in the hand of a warrior are the children of one's youth. Blessed is the man who fills his quiver with them" (Ps. 127:4–5). I have felt His abundant blessing.

TICKLING

I sometimes tell my patients that I am a pretty good doctor but one of the world's best at tickling. My patients come to expect the tickle. I usually sneak it in at the first visit. I end the exam with having them lift their arms as I count to see if all their ribs are there. By the second or third visit, they are already giggling when I get to that part. I come by this skill honestly, having been tickled ruthlessly by my father. Like all good family traditions, however, I have added significantly to the treasure chest of tickling strategies. For instance, I humbly avow that I invented the game of self-control. In this wonderful game, the subject lies on the floor with arms above shoulder level. In the first stage, the tickler is not allowed to touch the subject but can wiggle the fingers, rapidly go toward the ribs, and make fearsome tickling noises. Truly ticklish subjects cannot stand even this and will pull their arms down, showing a deplorable lack of self-control.

In the second stage, the tickler announces that he or she will now do easy tickles, touching allowed. The tickler then gently and softly caresses the ribs, not at all hard. Generally, the subject is convulsed with laughter but to demonstrate self-control must keep the arms up. This stage lasts just long enough to assure that self-control is, indeed, demonstrated.

The third stage separates the expert from the novice. This is the stage of hard tickles. After announcing that this time the ribs will indeed be thoroughly tickled, the subject is tickled with both hands, all the fingers, lots of tickling noises, and usually lots of encouragement from onlookers.

One day, while visiting Linda's family, I played self-control with Scott and Chris. They both demonstrated admirable control (by dint of much practice). To our surprise, Buddy, Linda's grandfather (about 75 at the time), said, "I want to try that."

"You mean you want to tickle Scott?" I asked.

"No," he asserted. "I want you to tickle me." He lay down on the floor, and after I went through stages 1 and 2, I asked, "Are you ready?"

"Yep," he said, and I really gave it to him. He roared, he laughed, he kicked his legs up and down, he shook all over—and he kept his arms up. My mother-in-law (Buddy's daughter) was in hysterics. We all were laughing, and I know we remember it because we reminisce occasionally. It is a unique memory about Buddy we all cherish.

In addition to self-control, tickling became part of some of our daily routines, at least for most of the children. Rachel was never a fan of tickling, letting me know she thought it an invasion of her personal space (even at age two she was very particular) and took days and days to forgive me if I did try to tickle her. So after a couple of tries, I gave up with her. Fortunately, she was the only one of the children to do that. Timo so loved tickling that at the ages of three and four, he would climb up on my lap, lie back on my knees, put his arms over his head, and command, "Daddy, tickle me!"

HOMESCHOOLING

"Dad, did I tell you about the play I'm in?" Scott asked me during an early morning jog.

"No, what kind of play is it?"

"It's a Halloween play. I am one of the witches' cats, and we go on strike. We make it so they can't fly on their broomsticks, and they have to give us what we want."

"How come you are in the play?" I asked.

"Everybody in class has to be in it." Scott didn't seem really excited to be in it, but he probably wouldn't have been excited to be in any play.

"Well, Scott, what do you think about this play? Actually, what I really want to know is what you think God thinks about the play."

We went home and looked up witches in the Bible. We also talked about godly authority and what it meant to go on strike against those God had put in authority over you. We talked about the message in the play. We prayed, and Scott said, "I don't think I want to be in this play."

"Okay," I said, "then you need to talk to your teacher."

The next week at a PTA meeting, Chris's teacher came up to Linda. "I just want you to know that if we ever have a play in class, I'll let you look at it before telling Chris he has to be in it." Linda was surprised. Chris's teacher must have heard about Scott's play, but she sure didn't hear it from us. We hadn't said anything to anyone. Next, Julie's mom came up to me. Julie was a classmate of Scott's, and her parents went to church with us.

"Jim, I heard you pulled Scott out of that play. We didn't like it, either, but decided not to make a fuss. What you did really challenged us, and I wish we had made a different decision. Thank you for doing that." I assumed she had heard about it from Julie. Then Linda ran into Scott's teacher.

"I let Scott out of the play," she said, "but I really think it is unreasonable of you to suggest that to him. You should not set the moral standards for your children. Parents need to let children decide for themselves."

I can only assume that it was okay for her, the teacher, to set moral standards, just not for parents.

That was the last year Scott and Chris were in public school. The next year, Scott would have been bussed far away, but even more importantly, our experience in public school, our growing concern about the focus of our children, and the school play experience made us consider other options. Certainly, a Christian school was an option, but a big part of our decision was that we felt we were losing our children's hearts. Although they spent a majority of their hours at home eating, sleeping, and doing chores, most of their social interactions were with peers and adults other than their parents. We noticed their conversations were often about things they didn't see at home. Their interactions with each other were flavored by the opinions of their friends, and conflicts among their friends were often brought home. It seemed clear they were being influenced greatly by their environment, and we were clearly losing the battle for their hearts. Homeschooling seemed the only option.

That year, the Florida legislature passed legislation that made it legal for the first time in that state to homeschool your children. The legislation had a two-year sunset provision. Unless actively renewed, it would expire after two years, so it was an experiment. We were the first homeschoolers we knew. In the years that followed, many others in our church and circle of friends began to homeschool as well, and it is now common. It certainly was not at that time.

For Linda, home-schooling required a rededication of her time. It has now been a focus of much of her efforts for many years, and the success of it in our family is a direct result of her dedication. While I have supported her, I have never had the time to be very involved in the day-to-day process. It has been a huge effort, tremendously costly in terms of time and energy. And it has been worth every moment of it.

Has homeschooling been worth it because the children have been academically advanced? No. In fact, they would have had more academic opportunities in public school, particularly with the development of the International Baccalaureate programs. In fact, I think science is particularly difficult to teach at home. Although the children have done well on standardized tests, it might well be that they would have done even better in public school.

Was homeschooling successful because it kept our children in a protected, nurturing environment during their formative years? Well, it did do that, and I think that has been important. Scott and Chris have a great relationship now, but they fought terribly when they both lived at home. Their relationship was a cause of significant strife in our home, and I think it was a pattern of behavior developed when they were in public school. Although our other children have had occasional disagreements, we have seen nothing like the conflict we saw with Scott and Chris. It is said that homeschooled children are adult-oriented rather than peer-oriented. Of course, some of our children have had significant peer orientation, probably from contact with peers in youth groups, sports teams, and neighborhood friends. But even with that difficulty, I think we can claim some success in that area. But that success is not the big reason I see homeschooling as worth it.

My children are not mine at all. They are God's children, given to me for a period—and for a purpose. Like the talents (money) given to the servants by the master, they have to be returned to God after a time. Like the master, God wants them to have grown and wants us to have been wise in our investing (read: parenting, in this context). What course of action can I take in regard to my children that is most likely to lead to God saying to me, "Well done, good and faithful servant" (Matt. 25:21)? Is it not to be faithful in every day, in education, in nurture, in discipline, in love, in protection, and in challenges until the day the job is complete and the child is a man or woman of God? That is ultimately why homeschooling is worth it. Simply put, it was the choice God gave us to raise a child for Him. Does that mean every parent who has ever sent a child to public school has chosen a poor path? Of course not, but I know I would have done so had I continued with that choice when God so clearly showed a better way for us.

Some of our grandchildren are homeschooled. Some would be if their circumstances were different. Some go to school outside the home because their parents think that is a better choice for them. None of our children have stated an objection to their own home-schooling past, but it doesn't have to be their choice for their children.

In the past, I have introduced myself as a fundamental, evan-gelistic Christian who brainwashes his children. The tendency of people who don't know me well is to immediately say, "Oh, I'm sure you're not really so bad." I don't know why they see that as bad. I believe in something strongly, I act on what I believe, and I do what I can to help my children see the same truth. My approach to father-hood is dominated by my faith in God and the work of Christ in my life. It all sounds pretty good to me.

FLIPPING AND FLYING

Scott loved to fly, a game where I took him outside and tossed him up into the air—only a little when he was young, but then higher and higher until he was up to the branches of the pines. Linda wouldn't watch. Scott would giggle and laugh and gasp as he was launched and caught. Chris liked it okay, but not as much as Scott. Timo was a great flyer and flipper because he was considerably smaller than Scott and Chris, an important factor. To do complicated flips, the children had to have enough neck muscle development to protect their necks and heads. Babies have disproportionately large heads and not enough muscle to have head control. That limits the gymnastics you can do with them. By the time Scott was old enough to have good head control, he was big enough that I couldn't do some things. Also, I was early in fatherhood and hadn't really developed my full routine.

I inherited flying from my dad. I probably flew some as a child, but I remember tossing my youngest brother, Bob, back and forth with Dad and seeing Bob tossed up and caught. I simply did the same. Timo, though, seemed to demand more. He loved the attention, was absolutely fearless, and loved to fly, so I began to experiment. I laid him on his back on my lap and flipped his legs up and over his head, landing him on the floor on his feet. He laughed and asked for more. He then started backing up a few feet before running to me, and I would catch him around the abdomen and flip him up in the air 270 degrees. I finished the move by catching him under his back and placing him on my lap, where he lay on his back, ready to start again. He would do this time after time. "More, Daddy, more! Again, Daddy, again!"

One time, I remembered a move I had seen and decided to try it. I stood and held Timo facing away from me on my arms with his legs straddling my forearms. I grabbed his arms between his legs, his right arm in my right hand, left in left. I gave him a gentle boost up, held his arms, and flipped his legs over his head before setting him on the ground. He loved it. I did the same and swung him back and forth between my legs. "More, Daddy, more!" I again did the flip, but this time after one swing between my legs I threw him up in the air, flipping his legs up in a 180-degree flip and then catching his legs. To finish it off, I gave another 180-degree flip, caught him under his arms, and set him down. "Do it again, Daddy. More, more!"

I picked him up and held him by the ankles, facing away from me, in a crouch, leaning back against my body. Then I nudged him forward, and he fell away from me, held firmly by the ankles. His upper body began swinging through my legs. On one forward swing, I gave a little more muscle and brought him all the way up, again resting against my body. What fun! Sometimes, on a forward swing I would let his feet go, and he would fly through the air to a waiting brother or uncle who caught him and sent him back the same way, back and forth, back and forth. It was a sad day for all of us when Timo got so big that he was in danger of hitting his head on the floor, and we had to quit.

Fortunately, the stream of potential Sherman flyers seemed endless. In succession, Kristin, Dorothy, and Ben flew and flipped. Rachel didn't. Like tickles, Rachel regarded flying and flipping as unreasonable intrusions on her personal space; she hated it and could not be persuaded otherwise. After a few tries, I gave up on her. Dorothy, like Timo, was a truly gifted flyer. Also relatively small, she thoroughly enjoyed the experience and spent much of her younger years in the air. She finally got too big, and we had to be very careful not to hit her head while swinging. One day I partly missed a catch, and she ended up on the floor. She wasn't hurt or even scared, but I was pretty shaken and decided Dorothy's flying days were over.

I am quite happy to note, however, that the tradition is being passed on. Aaron, Scott's son, showed promise as a flyer when Scott used the routines he learned at home. Scott sent me a picture of Aaron flying back and forth between Daddy and Uncle Chris in a pool. In one picture, he is flying to Chris, and the picture clearly shows uncertainty on his face, but the next picture shows him flying back to Scott with a look of serenity and joy. I have used these pictures in PowerPoint presentations to illustrate the result of working through a problem, from uncertainty to the joy and confidence of knowing you have solved a difficult dilemma. It gets the point across; plus, I get to show pictures of my family.

Outside of doing this at home, I am particularly fond of doing it at church. After the service is concluded and fellowship is going on, there are often little old ladies around doting on the children (as well they should; my children are indeed worth a little doting). When I do a fly-flip routine, the ladies gasp in wonder and delight, clutch their chests, close their eyes, and otherwise give me wonderful feedback. I'm sure it makes their day. Linda accuses me of base motives.

I got into trouble once, however. It was a Christmas gathering at our house, and my brother Mike was there with his wife, Carla, who had a challenging personality. Her marriage to Mike was short and rocky, but at this time, they seemed happy. Anyway, Carla was sitting on a couch, and Mike and I were in chairs facing each other across a coffee table. I caught Mike's eye and knew with absolute certainty he was thinking the same thing I was. He was ready. Kristin was sitting on my lap peacefully, facing me and snuggling quietly. I grabbed her under the arms, lifted her up, and sternly said, "Don't ever do that!" I then threw her away from me, right into the waiting hands of her uncle. He calmly caught her, settled her on his lap, and everything was fine—but not with Carla. When I threw Kristin, Carla at first started up off the couch in alarm, but she saw immediately that Kristin was safe with Mike and knew she had been had. She was not happy about it and ragged on Mike and me for a couple of hours. It pretty much ruined the evening. Mike and I still shake our heads about it; at the time, it seemed like a good idea, but maybe not.

I occasionally used to flip other people's children, though with a lot of care and little flamboyance. Sometimes they were scared, and I stopped immediately. Sometimes they loved it and asked for more. But real Sherman flipping is a learned skill and takes time to master. I'm now past the age where I can safely do it, but there are plenty of Sherman fliers around if you need a demonstration.

ACCIDENTS AND ILLNESSES

Active children and an active lifestyle will inevitably lead to trauma. When he was about a year old, Chris had his hand in the way of the door Scott was closing, and he lost the tip of one finger. Scott was pretty active at the time and often had bruises. One day, the chairman of my department, who was also my mentor, boss, and the kid's pediatrician, called me. "Shermie," he started, "where are you?"

"In the ICU."

"What are you doing there? It's 7:00 p.m."

"There are sick kids here; where do you think I should be?" I was chief resident at the time and pretty much in control. I didn't think anyone was as good a doctor as I was, and I ran the residency with an iron fist. I especially did not trust another physician to take good care of particularly sick children and made sure I knew about those patients first. (This was in my pre-Christian days, and I could be pretty tough.)

"Don't you think you're spending too much time there?" he asked.

I was a little puzzled. "That's why you pay me the big bucks. That's why you hired me," I responded.

"I wanted to talk to you about something and stopped by the house. Linda told me you were at the hospital. Scott had another big bruise on his forehead. Do you think there is any chance Linda is abusing the children?" He got right to the point. I explained Scott's active lifestyle, assured him all was well, and moved on.

Mostly, the trauma was pretty minor. Scott came into the house one time with his little finger pointing in an unusual direction. I thought he had dislocated it, and I tried to pop it into the joint.

I got it straight when I held it, but it kept returning to the abnormal position when I let go. After a couple of tries, he was interested in a different approach. It turned out to be broken and responded well to casting, but he reminds me of those well-meaning attempts from time to time when he wants to point out that I can be wrong.

Farming is said to be one of the most dangerous occupations. While we didn't operate farm equipment, we had opportunities to get hurt. During our life in Vermont, we heated the house with a woodstove and stored the wood in the garage. Every couple of weeks we worked through what was stored there and had to reload it, usually from stacks out in the woods. The horses pulled it to the house, and we stacked it. Often, the wood was not split, just cut into lengths. I kept an ax and a splitting maul with the wood and had carefully instructed the older boys in how to avoid maiming themselves when they split it, but mostly I split the wood. One day, Kenneth, about five years old, decided to try his hand with the ax. He first carefully instructed Kristin to stand behind him and then whacked her in the forehead on the back swing (or on the rebound from hitting the concrete floor; I never was sure how it happened). When Linda and I saw her, the whole side of her face was covered in blood, and we really couldn't see much else. Linda began sobbing. "Her eye, her eye! She'll never see again." I was trying to deal with two very frightened children, get the bleeding stopped, assess the damage, and decide what to do. I had little patience for hysteria. "Go into the other room and quit your wailing!" I commanded quite forcefully. I got Kristin cleaned up enough to see that the wound was in the forehead and through her eyebrow, but thankfully, her eye had been spared, and we went to the ER for stitches.

After we got home and everything had settled down, Linda approached me. "You weren't very gentle with me," she sniffed.

"No, I wasn't," I agreed. "But you were making a bad situation worse. One of these days I'm going to get hurt, and if you don't keep your head on, I may die. I need you to help, not hinder. This kind of thing is going to happen again; you need to respond better." I was still not very gentle. In retrospect, I recognize I could have made the point but soothed hurt feelings, too.

A couple of years later, the boys and I were carrying wood out of the shop and stacking it in a shed. The shop was full of stuff since Scott was rebuilding a truck, and engine parts were scattered everywhere. Timo, about 10 at the time, suddenly ran up to me. "Dad!" he announced with just a little quiver in his voice. "I just cut off my finger!"

He held up his hand and showed me. He had tripped while carrying a heavy board and hit his hand on the edge of a transmission. The wood on top and the metal edge under the hand had sheared through the distal joint of the fourth finger of his left hand.

Chris appeared. "I have the finger," he announced, helpfully.

I took Timo to the house. "Linda, Timo cut off his finger. Get me the first aid kit." She didn't say a word as she brought the kit.

"What do you want me to do with the finger?" She was ice-cold, nothing but business.

We wrapped the finger and cooled it, and then I took Timo and the finger to the hospital, where it was successfully reattached. The joint is gone, but the finger looks and works pretty normally. "How did I do this time?" she asked when I got back.

"Fantastic!" I encouraged her.

Although Linda has never had to save my life from an injury (at least not yet), she has had to minister to health needs in significant ways. In 2000, I discovered I had cancer in my kidney. I had a long surgical procedure with some complications and was pretty weak when I came home, and Linda was critically important in dealing with my needs. Scott, recognizing the situation, took off from work and stayed at the house for a week or two to do the cooking and shopping, take care of his younger brothers and sisters, and free Linda to concentrate on me. To do so, he left his family and work (with their blessing). I'm still touched by this effort to help. I then developed an infection in the surgical site, which required two subsequent surgeries, long courses of antibiotics, and eventually, an open incision requiring dressing changes twice a day. The gauze had to be put into the wound wet with saline, allowed to dry, and pulled out with each dressing change. The objective was to remove the infected debris and allow the wound to slowly scar closed. Linda had to change the dressings because pulling them out was very painful, and I couldn't do it myself. Kristin couldn't even watch. Rachel was pretty interested and would, I think, have been able to change them if Linda had not. Over a period of about three months, I slowly healed. Eventually, I got over it, having lost most, it seemed, of my muscle and all my stamina, but I began to recover. At first, I could only walk around the block. It took weeks before I could jog again, if only a little, and it was about two years before I felt back to full strength.

In church one Sunday when the congregation was asked about any praise reports, Timo announced, "I praise God because I see proof my dad is going to be okay. He got out the chainsaw yesterday and trimmed the trees." Another of the most gratifying moments in my recovery came when I felt strong enough to walk to the corner store and buy a bottle of Diet Coke. Linda had decided my cancer was because of the chemicals in Diet Coke and had cut me off. "Is there anything I can do for you?" she would ask sweetly.

"Give me some Diet Coke," I would plead.

"No!" she would say. "Anything other than that?" She finally broke down and bought a 20-ounce bottle, limiting me to two ounces per day.

Linda's strength, compassion, and attention to me during this time were amazing. I got far better care from her than I would have gotten if I had remained in the hospital. Her love and concern were as important in the healing process as the medications and treatments. Helping in the process as well were the prayers of many friends and family. My colleagues at work covered for me and supported me through the time without complaint. I never required radiation or chemotherapy, and more than 20 years later, I have normal evaluations. I am, apparently, a surgical cure and grateful for the extra time I will have with my family.

We were open with the children about my problem, discussing the options and the possible outcomes. If they were emotionally scarred from the experience, I have never detected it. I think they understood the gravity, but as Linda and I did not panic, I think they gained confidence that the outcome was in God's hands and we could trust Him. We seldom talk about my cancer or the difficult time after the surgery. It isn't avoided, but we simply regard it as a trial from which we learned and grew.

These are certainly not the end of the illnesses or trauma. In a previous essay, I mentioned Karin, our child with trisomy 21 who died during surgery for her severe congenital heart malformation. We prayed for healing, and God saw fit to heal her in His own way. Kenneth served in the Iraq War and saw things that bothered him greatly, but he grew spiritually with the experience. I have needed many more surgeries, mostly orthopedic, but am doing well. In all these times, we are strengthened in our faith and dependence on one another. I thank God daily for the incredible grace and protection He has given our family.

SKIING

Our son Chris graduated with a degree in accounting from the University of Florida. As he considered life beyond college, he developed a clear list of priorities: skiing. It was a short list. He thought it would also be nice to have a job that used his college degree since making enough money to support himself would be a nice perk. But the absolute necessity was that it would allow him to ski, and the best place for that was clearly in the Rockies. He got a job as an accountant at a ski resort west of Denver and never regretted the decision.

We had our opportunity to ski when we moved to Vermont in 1988. We bought a house in a very rural community about 45 minutes from Smugglers' Notch and an hour from Jay Peak, both large ski resorts in northern Vermont. Chris and Scott skied with a homeschooling group for a very reasonable charge. Downhill skiing is pretty expensive, but if you live in the area, at least you can choose days when the conditions are good. I pretty rapidly learned that skiing with Scott and Chris was dangerous. Attempting to keep up with them, I went off a trail and took a direct hit in the mouth on a trail marking post. Another day I took a mogul, got off-balance, and landed on my head and shoulder. I think I dislocated a rib—it was pretty painful for a time.

As Timo and Kenneth got older, they began to ask about learning to ski. We had done some cross-country skiing, so they had been on skis and were excited to try downhill. My clearest memory of Kenneth's first day is seeing him rocket down a hill in a crouched position, completely out of control. I had started him out in a snowplow across the face of the hill. He got a few feet from me, his skis got parallel, and he turned down the hill. As he picked up speed, I started screaming at him to fall down, but he was so far down in a crouch that he was kind of stuck there. I was afraid he would hit someone and terrified he would go off the trail into the trees. I could see all kinds of disasters looming large. He was going really fast when he finally managed to topple over into a huge explosion of snow, legs, and skis. Although a little shaken, he was otherwise okay. I got a lot more careful after that. Generally, I would ski down the hill backward, bent over, holding the tips of Kenneth's skis together, and telling him to keep his heels out. After a few trips, the kids usually caught on. If they didn't, well, at least I was downhill between them and disaster.

Timo is older than Kenneth and took to skiing as though it were second nature. The first day I took him was a day we had been planning for a couple of weeks. We went to Smugglers' Notch, and Scott and Chris skied with us a little but mostly were off on their own. Timo and I started on a green and moved rapidly to the blues. He did very well and seemed to be enjoying himself a lot. It was a cold day, around 0 degrees, and cloudy with a blustery wind. Fog was in the air most of the day, and the moisture just made it colder. Our clothes got a layer of ice that cracked when we moved, and my beard rapidly turned white with ice. We would warm up with the exercise of skiing down the hill and then get cold as we rode a lift back up the mountain. Up on the lifts, there was no shelter from the wind. The seats and stanchions were ice-encrusted, and when the attendants had to stop the lift to help a struggling skier, we hoped they would get going pretty soon. Toward the end of the day, we had been skiing for about six hours and were tired and more than a little cold. As we sat on an unmoving ski lift, buffeted by a piercing wind, Timo looked up at me and said, "Dad, thanks for taking me skiing. I'll remember this day for the rest of my life."

"So will I, Timo, so will I." It suddenly didn't seem nearly so cold.

Most of the skiing we did was cross-country. We lived far out in the country in an area that was mostly woods, mountains, and dairy farms. The Vermont Association of Snow Travelers is a very active organization that maintains an extensive trail system. After it snows, a member grooms the trails by pulling a heavy sled behind a snowmobile. The trails are well maintained, clearly marked, and challenging since snowmobilers like turns and hills. Cross-country skiers are allowed to use the trails without charge; they just have to get to the side when a snowmobile comes along. These trails seem to go forever, certainly much farther than we could ever go in a day. There were trails near our house, and we frequently went out to ski on them.

The woods are quiet in the winter. Without leaves on the trees, you can see much farther. The trees protect you from the wind, and the contrast and patterns of the bark of the trees against the pure white snow create a picture I love. I also liked the exercise. You can exercise as much or as little as you like depending on how far and how fast you go. Beyond the equipment, the activity also costs nothing. Our dogs loved the outdoors and loved going with us on ski excursions. When the snow turned to ice between their toes, they would pause at the side of the trail, bite it out, and rejoin us. Cross-country skis are not really made for turning, though, and these trails put a premium on turns. The kids and I saw who could go the longest without falling down, and it was rare that anyone could get through the day without a spill.

We loved Vermont. I had more time to spend with my family than at any other time of my life, and we spent that time doing lots of different things. We loved the lifestyle. We especially loved winter and were outside in it a great deal. We were disappointed when it warmed up and spoiled our snow or melted the ice on the pond. About a year after we moved back to Florida, I saw Kristin sitting under a tree looking pensive. "What's up?" I asked.

"I miss Vermont," she said. I think we all did.

Maple Ridge, our home in Virginia, is about an hour's drive from Snowshoe, West Virginia. Chris and his family have a one-bedroom condo there, and they ski frequently. Their two girls are rapidly becoming excellent skiers. During maple syrup season, we usually take a break or two, and everyone who wants to do so goes to Snowshoe for a day of skiing. It makes for a long day, but for the families who live in Florida, it is apparently worth it. Linda and I are far past our skiing days, so we watch the babies, cook, and make sure the hot chocolate is warm and plentiful.

IT ISN'T FAIR

"That isn't fair!"

Most parents have heard their child say this, usually when a decision is made that limits the child's actions. I recently heard one of my grandchildren say this to his parent. The parent's response in turn indicated that the child had made a reasonable observation, and the parent would try to be fairer. I didn't intervene, knowing it wasn't appropriate to do so. Trying to parent your grandchildren and instruct their parents in the moment seems like a good way to overstep and offend. So I wrote this essay and sent it out. I got no response from anyone.

"It isn't fair!" is often followed by a justification for the charge. "Johnny got to go, and so should I." It is natural for parents to want their children and the larger community of church, school, and neighborhood to see them as fair.

The dictionary lists many meanings for *fair*, but the one most applicable to this discussion is "free from bias, dishonesty, or injustice."[1] There is no indication in the dictionary definition that fair is synonymous with equal. It is certainly possible to be fair without being equal, but the unequal treatment needs to be on the basis of something other than favoritism.

The concept of unequal treatment being unfair is common in children, but it is often seen in adults as well. As I deal with illness, I often hear "it just isn't fair" when someone discovers they have a challenging illness—one they never anticipated, one that may end

---

1. "Fair," Dictionary.com, https://www. dictionary. com/browse/fair.

their life before their expectation. This concept is based on the implicit expectation that parents or God or fate owes equal treatment to everyone. That is a flawed concept.

The Declaration of Independence states, "We hold these truths to be self-evident, that all men are created equal, that they are endowed by their Creator with certain unalienable Rights, that among these are Life, Liberty, and the pursuit of Happiness."[2] The equality here, I think, is of equal value in the world, equally special to God, equally loved by God, or equal in sinfulness and the need for a relationship with God. It is not an equality of height, eye color, intelligence, opportunity, life span, degree of happiness, earning potential, or any of the other measures we often use to assess the quality of life. In parallel, children have certain rights that are self-evident such as the right to an equal portion of their parents' love, protection, provision, discipline, and nurturing.

In ethics, there is a principle of justice in which justice has to do with the equitable distribution of resources. When the resource is abundant with more than enough for everyone, there is little conflict, and everyone takes what they want. But when the resource becomes limited and there is not enough for everyone to take all they want, the ethics of justice are important. Within different political viewpoints, the distribution system can look quite different. To everyone according to what they earn, to everyone according to their ability to pay—these lead to quite different distribution systems, but no distribution system can be considered ethical if its basis is to everyone according to whom they know or to the person who offers me the largest bribe. In the context of parenting, love should not be a limited resource, but food, shelter, or protection might be. Their distribution, when limited, must be equitable. God calls on fathers to self-sacrificially make those decisions. It would

---

2. "The Declaration of Independence," Ushistory.org, https://www. ushistory. org/ declaration/document/.

never be fair or just to distribute a full meal to the favorite child while others starve.

Is God ethical? Fortunately for us, He does not give us what we deserve based on our works. He offers us so much more based on His works on our behalf. He operates out of love for us even when we are steeped in sin. That offer of forgiveness is available to everyone; if some refuse it, their outcome is not unfair. If some accept it late in a life filled with hate and anger, it is not unfair that they were forgiven for so much; it is a cause for celebration. (I am very aware of the apparent contradiction in scripture of predestination versus free will. Please do not make an assumption of my theological bent based on this discussion.)

As parents, we need to teach our children that life is not fair, but God is just. Life does not treat us equally, but it can be filled with joy. We cannot always treat our children equally, but the unequal treatment must be based on something other than unequal love or unequal commitment to their well-being. It isn't a lesson easily learned by a three-year-old, but it is a lesson a 30-year-old should have learned long ago. Life isn't fair is accurate as an observation, but it should never be a complaint.

I have not always treated my children equally. Some graduated from college with debt and others without it. Some had their education covered by scholarships or a salary supplement granted by my employer, and others had my post-tax income. One child got a new car during college; others drove used cars that were certainly not sporty. I once asked a couple of children if those differences bothered them. The response was something like this: "No, not at all. You supported each of us as well as you were able to at the time. Over the 20 years you had children in college, the circumstances varied. There was no favoritism involved." Helping them through college is far from the only time there was unequal treatment, but the help I gave was always dependent on the need I perceived and my ability to meet it. I felt no compunction to be equal. If I felt the need to send $100 to one child, I did it and never thought I needed to send $100 to every other child. I know some families do this, and I have considered it, but I decided it was not the way for us to go. I think my decision has never been a problem.

So, having thought this through, how would I respond to a child's complaint that my decision about something was not fair? If time to respond was limited, I might say, "I can see how you might think it isn't fair, and we will talk about it later. But for right now, please know that I'm not just being mean, and the decision is final." If I had plenty of time, I might ask, "Why do you think it isn't fair? What does it mean to be fair? Can you think of any reasons that Daddy might have made that decision?" and go on from there. I doubt I handled this issue that well at the time my own children raised the complaint, but I am sure my children felt I loved them all. I have heard them say, "I know Daddy loves you a lot, but he loves me the most." As long as each one of them thinks I love them the most, I'm okay with that.

JOGGING

Scott, Chris, and I were jogging through the back roads of Lutz, Florida, on a hot Sunday during the summer. We often went right after church on Sundays, although we showed more sense during the rest of the week and went early in the morning. I would describe Chris as an unenthusiastic jogger, and that would probably overestimate his desire to run with me. So maximum effort was not a characteristic of his approach; complaining was. I never really knew how much he was capable of doing, so I generally required him to run but let him control the pace. On this particular day, he was going quite slowly, so much so that I was having a hard time controlling my irritation. In the midst of telling myself to have patience and enjoy the day, I heard him exclaim, "Hey, look! I can walk faster than we are running!" This was one of those times when someone says something and immediately knows it was a mistake. If they could reach out, grab the last word, and immediately stuff the sentence back in their mouth, they would.

"Oh really?" I exclaimed. "Well, we can certainly fix that." I picked up the pace right away. Chris still remembers that as one of the stupidest things he's ever said.

Jogging became a family tradition when Scott was about seven years old. We were living in Lutz, and I was a new associate professor in the Department of Pediatrics at the University of South Florida. Twice a week I got up early and played handball. But that wasn't enough exercise for me, so I got up early a couple more times a week and ran about three miles, mostly to increase my endurance for handball. One day Scott asked, "Dad, can I run with you?" To be

45

honest, I wasn't all that excited at the offer; he was clearly not going to keep the pace I needed for training. But doing something with Scott was the fatherly thing to do, so I said, "Sure." We started out with about a mile-and-a-half jog at a pretty slow pace, but he liked it. I only got him up once the first week, but he was disappointed about that, so I gave up on training and decided it was time for fathering instead. After about a month, we were up to three miles, and he still seemed to enjoy it. One day during our run, I asked, "Scott, do you want to train with me to run a road race? It will mean we have to slowly increase our distance and run on other days, too." He agreed, and that February, we ran in the Gasparilla Classic. There are two races the same day, a 5K and a 15K. We ran the 15K. We ran to finish, for the personal satisfaction of training for and accomplishing something challenging, and to do something together. Because there were so few children his age, I think he took a medal in the age category, which went up to 14. The next year, he ran again and did even better.

The year after that, it became a family tradition. Chris was now seven years old, and I decided he should be part of this. He didn't get a choice in the matter, and he never liked it, thus the episode mentioned earlier. He ran the 15K that year, but I think that was the last year he did. Scott and Chris did compete in some triathlons in subsequent years, but rugby was much more to Chris's liking than running. A neighbor once asked Scott and Chris, "How does it feel to grow up in an army boot camp?" I think it was a reference to running in the early morning.

Timo was just six years old when we moved to Vermont. During the six years we lived there, he did run with me some, including a race of about 10K in St. Albans. When we moved back to Florida in 1994, we moved to McIntosh, a small town south of Gainesville. I started jogging again and immediately involved my children in the activity. While I am willing to run by myself, I much prefer company. Timo was a willing participant; Kenneth was not. Timo was perfectly willing to do almost anything if he could do it with me, but Kenneth only wanted to do what he wanted to do. I would not have thought anyone could be less enthusiastic about jogging than Chris, but Kenneth proved me wrong. In 1995, Kenneth, Timo, and I ran the 15K Gasparilla. They were older than Scott and Chris, and I was older, too. By this time, I was having a hard time keeping up, particularly with Timo.

Kristin, Rachel, and Dorothy each in turn had their opportunity. So did Ben when he was six or seven. Kristin developed an overuse injury to her knee that seemed to never heal, and she couldn't run the Gasparilla. Rachel, Dorothy, and Ben ran together one year, taking a first and two seconds in their age groups.

As I write this, I still run occasionally with the younger children. We have found a trail through the woods near our house in Roanoke and run about two-and-a-half miles. Rachel is not a good runner since she overstrides and generally hates it. Dorothy is a natural with an effortless stride, fast turnover, and lots of stamina. Unfortunately, she, too, has some knee problems. Ben runs pretty well and seems to enjoy it. I have developed arthritis in one knee, and it hurts to run, but I still love running with the children.

I think jogging together has been good for us. Kristin never particularly enjoyed running; in fact, she has vomited many times along the streets of McIntosh. But during her freshman year of college, she wrote a paper about how she hated the running I made her do and how much she wished she could run the Gasparilla with me. During one period, I required the kids to run with or without me. As I tended to push them, they preferred without. When I got home each day, they were always already headed out the door, so I couldn't say, "Hey, wait a minute for me to change, and I'll go with you."

Ben doesn't remember a time when Scott and Chris lived with us. Toward the end of when we lived in McIntosh, Timo and Kenneth were in college and not around much. That left Ben in the house with Linda, Kristin, Rachel, and Dorothy. Since we homeschooled, there was no interaction during most of the day with boys his age, and there were almost no boys his age in town. I didn't think much about the effect this might be having on him until one day I asked him, "So, how did your jog go today?"

"I didn't run today," he answered.

"Why not?" I asked. "Today is a running day."

"I know," he said, "but I had a headache and cramps."

I was pretty taken aback. I had heard my daughters say they couldn't run because of cramps, and when I had suggested they shouldn't let a little thing like that get in the way of something important like running, I got into serious trouble with Linda. But hearing this from my son was a first for me. At dinner that night I announced, "Ben told me he was unable to run today because of cramps and a headache." There was silence as those possessing high levels of estrogen chewed over that information and waited for what was sure to follow. "I don't like what you are doing to my son," I growled. Protestations of innocence followed, but the fact speaks for itself. Headache and cramps, indeed!

SUGARING

I have always had an affinity for growing things and using what the land provides. I love to garden and particularly love growing vegetables. I like doing things that have a useful outcome beyond ornamentation. I like trees. The thought of having trees and using them to get nuts, heat, or lumber is attractive. Sugaring, the Vermont term for maple syrup production, is a natural attraction. When we moved to Vermont, one of the partners in the practice I joined owned about 60 acres of land. The spring after we moved there, he invited us to participate in sugaring. We tapped the trees, hung buckets, collected the sap, watched as it boiled down, and enjoyed the syrup. We spent a lot of time that first year with that family, and much of it involved sugaring. When we bought our own property after about a year, we had sugar maples on most of the 20 acres. Down the road from our house was a large sugar house owned by a neighbor who had about 5,000 taps of his own and let us bring our sap to his sugar house. He boiled it down and gave us some syrup in exchange. By the second year, Scott and Chris were working for him, going with him to tap the trees, putting together the pipeline, stacking the wood, helping him collect sap, and generally involving themselves in the whole process. The other children often visited the sugar house, and our neighbor seemed to enjoy having them around. Before he hired Scott and Chris, I think this neighbor had had a hard time finding reliable help; there was never any question about Scott and Chris working for him after the first year even though at first they were pretty young.

About the last four years we were there, Scott and Chris tapped our trees in a serious way. We had two draft horses, Dick and Bud, and they hitched them to our sled or wagon and went out to gather sap. The first year they did it, they tapped trees that were a long way from the trails the horses could travel on and spent 14 to 16 hours per day gathering sap and walking up hills about an eighth of a mile carrying five-gallon buckets of sap. Those were some tired boys. The next year, they didn't bite off quite as much—learning from your mistakes is a useful life skill. I was pretty busy during sugaring season, so I couldn't help much.

After a couple of years, Scott decided he wanted to do this on his own. He was about 17 at the time, six feet tall, and a rock-hard 180 pounds. He could do man's work and go pretty much all day. One day he found a sugar bush that hadn't been tapped in years and contacted the owner. I happened to be present during part of the telephone conversation, and hearing Scott's part of it, I realized the owner was reluctant to let Scott lease the land. He finally asked to talk to me and didn't waste time jumping into the conversation. "Scott wants to lease my land," he said.

"Yes, I know. He talked it over with me," I replied.

"I understand he is 17."

"Yes, that's right," I acknowledged. "But he is very responsible and will take good care of your land. He has been working with our neighbor and knows about sugaring. The neighbor has told him that he will help him if he has problems," I tried to reassure him.

"In order for this to work for me, the lease has to be for a number of years. You can't do this for just one season," he said.

I thought he was worried that Scott wouldn't be able to do the work. "Scott is a good worker," I stated. "He won't walk away from this if he commits to do it."

"Oh, that's not the problem," he protested. "Everybody in Franklin County knows about your boys and how they work. I'm worried he will decide to go to college and not be here for sugaring after this year."

Eventually, it didn't work out to lease the property because the owner wanted an unreasonable amount of money. To me, though, the memorable part was the exclamation that everybody in the county knew about Scott and Chris and their work ethic. We had never met this man, but he knew of their reputation. I have a hard time thinking of something as satisfying for a father to hear about his children.

Another sugaring moment happened one year when I was tapping our trees. The horses were out in the woods with us, hitched to the wagon. In the wagon were the pails and covers we hung on the spouts. That year there was still a lot of snow cover in the woods, but the day wasn't particularly cold, probably in the 30s. The snow was up to my waist and had a thick crust on top. The crust made it harder to get through, and it wasn't nearly strong enough to walk on. Scott and Chris were working somewhere else, so I was tapping with the younger kids. I had a gas-operated drill, a hammer, and a pouch full of taps. I drilled the hole, Kenneth hammered in the tap, and Timo hung the bucket and put on the covers. The snow was so deep that Kenneth and Timo couldn't get through it by themselves; they had to walk where I had opened the path. For Kenneth, it was relatively easy, as he just stayed with me. For Timo it was a much bigger challenge. He could carry only four to five buckets and covers at a time and then had to go back to the wagon for more. I, on the other hand, could just go from tree to tree, tapping as I went until I thought we needed to move the wagon. Dick and Bud just stood there, patiently waiting. Timo had to keep retracing his steps; he couldn't go in a direct line to the wagon.

Timo had a blue stocking cap that was pretty stretched out and kept falling over one eye. He was up to his shoulders in the snow, going as fast as he could back and forth to the wagon, struggling to keep up. I kept an eye on him and tried to tap at a pace he could handle.

"Are you okay, Timo?" I asked.

"I'm great, Dad!" he exclaimed, a big grin on his face and absolutely radiating joy from every fiber of his being. "I can keep up; don't worry about me."

As much as I love the aspect of harvesting from the goodness of the land, the best thing about sugaring was the family time—being out in the woods working together, each contributing to the task, spending time together in a beautiful setting, accomplishing something in addition to the time together. That is my love language. The children know that spending time talking to Linda is what she cherishes. For me, it is working together. Sugaring together, in fact, became the driving force for Maple Ridge.

MAPLE RIDGE

Moving from Vermont to Florida was a wonderful opportunity but had a downside; we had to leave a lifestyle and environment we loved. The first two years after the move, we drove back to Vermont for our vacations, one during the summer and one during the winter. The winter vacation was interesting. We stayed at a friend's house, took care of their animals, milked the goats, did the chores, and skied at Smugglers' Notch while they took their first vacation together in many years. But Vermont is about 36 hours from Gainesville, so the next year we did a camping trip in West Virginia. While we were there, we discovered you can do sugaring in that area (there is a fair abundance of sugar maples likely because of the altitude). Reading in a brochure about the area, we discovered that Highland County, Virginia, has a yearly maple syrup festival and advertises itself as the farthest south in the USA where you can regularly tap trees for syrup. We subsequently learned there are large producers there with more than 10,000 taps.

Virginia seemed like a good place to look for land for eventual retirement. Because it is more central in the eastern United States, it would likely be more easily accessible to the children and to us. Also, the tax structure in Vermont is unfriendly to landowners who are not residents. For the next five years, we made almost yearly visits to Highland County to look at property, meet with real estate agents, and explore. We found beautiful property we couldn't afford, property so steep we couldn't walk it, property next door to the town dump, and property with houses already built. Then one Christmas, Chris's mother-in-law sent us a container of maple syrup from Eagle's

Sugar Camp in McDowell, Highland County. An accompanying note said, "I saw this and thought of you; I guess your dream of sugaring with your grandchildren could become reality after all."

I wrote a letter to Mr. Eagle's Sugar Camp, telling him about our family and our dream. I received a note back saying he had no property for sale but would keep his eyes open. In March, in the local newspaper there was a full-page real estate advertisement and a crayon-circled ad describing Maple Cove. I called. The agent hadn't walked the property but promised to do so and call me back. I learned it had a stream, no buildings, perimeter fencing, and mature maple trees, enough to tap for a family but not a commercial operation. It was 85 acres with about 30 open acres and the rest in hardwoods. It had lots of road frontage. Linda and I flew up, rented a car, met the agent in Monterey, and spent about four hours on the property. It was the end of winter, there were no leaves on the trees, and it was cloudy and blustery. We loved the land and signed an offer immediately. The next day, the agent called to say the seller had accepted the offer.

A local farmer owned the land. He was born in Highland County and did a little of everything. He had an auction barn, raised cattle, scouted timber for sawyers, played harmonica, spun yarns, and had an infectious laugh. When excited, which was often, he rubbed his palms together. He had owned the land for about 20 years, having bought it as an investment for when he retired, and wanted the land to go to someone who would love and appreciate it. I think he was satisfied after he met our family.

The first time we vacationed on the property was later that year, in 2000. We rented a class C camper in Roanoke and stayed on the property. I had arranged to have an excavating company do the initial perk test, and while we were there, they came to look at the property and make suggestions about a building site, water, and driveway. The owner of Spruce Hill Excavating Company met us there. He suggested a site for the house, talked about how to develop the spring, and suggested a route for the driveway. With Linda's approval, we agreed, and he started putting in the spring while we were there. I got out the chain saw and helped. Also on that trip I found a used mobile home nearby, bought it, and arranged to have it put on the land, have a septic tank installed, and get the water hooked up. On our next trip there, we stayed in the trailer and did so from then until the basement of the house was finished.

The first building project was a picnic table Timo and Kenneth built with wood from a local sawmill. The next one was a storage shed near the trailer, and the next structure was the sugar house where we would make the maple syrup.

We bought this property thinking it would eventually be a place the family could come to enjoy nature, relax, and be together. I was thinking that would happen after we were permanently living there, after the house was built. However, as we began to develop the land and build the preliminary structures, I realized it was already happening. Our children and their families participated in the various projects. They were interested and available, sometimes a few, sometimes many. The trailer was often so crowded at night that we had to step carefully on the way to the bathroom; sometimes it was just Linda and me. But almost immediately, the land became what it was intended to be—a place of community, family, working together, relaxation (occasionally), and good times. Linda polled the family, and we named it Maple Ridge.

When I finally recovered from my cancer surgery and the following complications and had a heightened sense of my age and potential mortality, I decided that if I was ever going to build a house at Maple Ridge, I had better get started, and doing it from Gainesville was not going to work. I found a job in Roanoke, Virginia, about two hours from Maple Ridge and moved the family there. At that time, three daughters and a son lived with us; the rest were grown and gone. In 2006, we began building. In 2017, I retired so I could work full-time on the house, and in 2019, it was finally finished (if any owner-built house is ever finished). This has been an enormous project but one in which Linda and each of the children have had a part. It has been a project that would be too big for me to try to bite off now; my timing on this one was about right. I hope many generations of Shermans use this as a place of relaxation and peace. I'll put some pictures on the walls to help them tell their grandchildren how they helped build it.

Of course, the initial vision of Maple Ridge was to make it a place for the family to make maple syrup. In the spring of 2009, we finally finished enough of the house so we could stay in it during the winter. The trailer was never winterized, and the pipes would freeze if there was water in them. There was no heat system except a kerosene portable heater, which was inadequate for anything more than mild heating. However, the house had a good heating system, and once we got enough of it constructed, we hauled the trailer off the site and moved our operations to the house. That spring I polled the children. "There is enough money to do any one of several things, but not enough for all of them. Do I concentrate on finishing the house or getting ready to sugar?" It was unanimous: sugar. We built a pole barn where the trailer had been, and when it was completed, we emptied the sugar house of all the equipment stored in it. I had acquired an evaporator, but it was old and rusty and missing parts. I contacted Leader Evaporator and spoke to a salesman who helped me decide on which size evaporator to buy and what additional equipment I would need. When we got around to shipping, I was nervous about what it would cost. However, the salesman had a daughter who lived in southwest Virginia and visited her each year. He said he could load the order on his truck and deliver it. On Labor Day weekend, he showed up and spent the day with us getting the evaporator set up and helping lay out a pipeline in the woods. The following spring, our children and grandchildren showed up. We tapped trees, ran the evaporator, and made 13 gallons of syrup. It was literally a dream come true. We have sugared each of the subsequent years. Each of my children has had this experience with their families, and everybody enjoys the syrup.

BUILDING A TIMBER FRAME

W hen people discovered I was building a house with my family, they wondered how I developed those skills, usually assuming I learned them from my father. Actually, it was Linda's father, Rip, who got me started when he helped me remodel our first house. Then, over the years and through multiple moves, there were projects that needed other tools and other skills. Gradually, I accumulated enough of each that I thought I could tackle building a new house. Over time, I made mistakes, recognized them, and learned from them. I did not think I could build a house without making any mistakes, but I thought I could overcome them. That confidence was built on experience and was, perhaps, the most critical element I brought to the project. Also, I had children who could help.

Scott had worked with a house builder for a couple of years after high school and learned a lot. The other children worked with me on various projects and learned to cut, drive a nail, screw, and measure. After the oldest boys left home, the first thing I built with only girl help was the deck outside the trailer at Maple Ridge. I had never built a deck, so I bought a book, read it, designed the deck, and ordered the materials. The girls carried the lumber, learned how to use a circular saw, and helped me measure. They countersank and drove all the screws to hold the deck down. They were great help, enjoyed their participation, and felt a sense of accomplishment with the job. I never heard a peep from them that this really isn't something girls should be doing. If you looked through the pictures of building the sugar house and main house, you would see girl power clearly demonstrated.

Linda and I developed the idea of building a house at Maple Ridge even before we found the land; although, the idea was pretty undeveloped. We knew it needed to be a house with open spaces, a place that would be comfortable with just two people or with 30 people. We knew it should be easy to maintain, have lots of windows, and lend itself to community activities while giving some opportunity for privacy when needed. We toyed with standard construction, with log homes, and with timber frame construction. Finally we settled on timber frame. Timo and I spent a week at Cowee Mountain Timber Framers in Cowee Mountain, North Carolina, working in their shop. We learned to read the shop drawings, make cuts, and use the specialized tools. After we moved to Roanoke, my brother Mike spent three months at Cowee Mountain working in the shop, doing design work, and finally going on what's called a raising.

After a lot of discussion about the priorities for the house, Linda and I adapted a design we had found in a log home package to a timber frame structure and contacted Cowee Mountain about cutting our frame. Again, we went through a negotiation, a consultation with an engineering firm, and then a contract. Our frame was cut in the fall of 2004 and delivered to Maple Ridge. We stickered and stacked the beams, covered them with tarps, and waited for the foundation to be built. The foundation was poured in the late spring of 2005, and we got the floor trusses up and covered that fall. The frame sat through another winter, and in the spring of 2006, we thought we were ready to try to do a raising.

Cowee Mountain offers to do the raising for you for a considerable price. Mike and I thought we could do it, although we felt uncertain. We had shop drawings of the structure, but there were no instructions for putting it together. Where do you start? Do you try to build pieces on the ground and then lift them in place, or do you stand up a pole and add one piece at a time? There are places where three or four big pieces of lumber all join. Which ones go in first, or does it matter? We got sticks and dowels, drilled holes in them, and talked about it. Mike developed confidence that we could do it, and I trusted him. I should note that although my brain is pretty good in many areas, I do not have much ability to see in three dimensions. I cannot visualize structures well. I think all my family is much better at that. We rented a boom forklift, had it delivered, took two weeks of vacation, and set to work.

At the beginning of the raising, I had some anxiety about how this was going to go. I had $45,000 invested in the timber frame structure, had rented the equipment, and was going ahead without really knowing if we could do it or how long it would take. Also, we were gambling on the weather. Storms and lots of rain would make the ground so slippery that we might not get much done. My hope was that we would have it together by the end of the two weeks and that no one would get hurt in the process. If I could have been guaranteed those two things, I would have been a happy man. In fact, we had only one rainy day, no one got hurt, and we accomplished almost everything in the two weeks. We were able to finish the part that required the forklift and handled the rest a couple of weekends later.

Initial progress was slow. We sometimes made errors and had to take out beams and fix our mistakes. In one section, we did things in the wrong order and didn't support a long, horizontal beam correctly. It sagged, making the rafters fit poorly. When we discovered the error, we were able to use a hydraulic jack to lift the sagging beam and correct the problem. Three beams were cut incorrectly, and it took time to discover why we had gotten out of square. It was easy to fix once we found the problem. Having gone through the process once, it would go much faster if we had another similar frame to construct. Had we hired professional help, the work might have gone faster, but it certainly would have cost more. Our frame was a custom one, very different from standard timber frame construction that uses bents. Professionals might have avoided some of the mistakes we made but probably would not have built one just like ours. Having someone else do the job might have been faster, but we would have missed what turned out to be one of the really wonderful parts of the project.

Watching that structure rise up into the sky was exciting. During the first week, there were a number of days when only Chris and his wife, Kara, were there with Mike and me. Since no one had experience with heavy machinery except Mike (and we needed him to help fit in the beams), Kara seemed a good choice to drive the forklift. She was intelligent, precise, careful, and had never done anything like that before. The latter fact made her depend totally on the directions we gave her using hand signals, making her safe. After a brief period of training, she was our machine operator. She had a blast, contributed greatly to the project, and was excited at the whole experience. When Scott and his wife, Tracy, came the next week, Tracy took over the machine, leaving childcare (Aaron, Nathan, and Emily) to the aunts (Rachel, Kristin, and Dorothy). She also had a great time. It occurred to me that if my daughters-in-law were an important part of the process and enjoyed the time there, they would likely have more enthusiasm about continuing to visit and working with me. I think we accomplished that goal as well.

The Highland County building inspector visited one day. He was in the area and decided to drop by to check out our progress. He is not a big talker. After wandering around the building site for a time, he came to me. "Interesting," he said, and paused. "Don't see many like this." He might have been referring to timber frame construction, but perhaps he meant having children on a building site, or young women driving construction equipment, or no safety harnesses on the people 30 feet in the air balanced on eight-inch-wide beams while driving wooden pegs into joints, or no hard hats anywhere on the site. But I think he meant timber frame. "Doing it with family, huh? Don't see that much anymore. Interesting." He didn't offer any critical comments and passed us on the inspection, so I guess "interesting" was within the building code.

Linda's participation in these projects was also critical. She modified my ideas so much that they became more hers than mine. My first concept for the house was about 1,600 square feet; hers was 4,300. The final design was 4,200, which is some indication of who tends to prevail in these negotiations. When people visit and are impressed at the house, they like the timber frame structure, but they also like the decorative touches, the color selections, the complicated lighting scheme, and the thoughtful placement of light switches and outlets. All of them were Linda's work product. Although the walls are plumb and the studs are accurately on 16-inch centers (my work product), that's not what people see. The final product is very clearly a result of a team effort. Sometimes I may say, "I built this house," but the truth is that we built it.

I have often mentioned to Linda that our objective in buying the land was to build a place where the children and their families would visit and spend time with us. We envisioned a house and barn, animals, a pond, mountains, fresh air, paintball games, and four-wheelers. I should have anticipated (but did not) that the fellowship, the visits, and the joy of working together would start almost immediately, as we worked together building the structures we would one day use. The sugar house, the shed, the picnic table, the deck on the trailer, and now the house are all projects in which the children participated. Their handprints are all over these things, and I see the day coming when I hear them explain to their children how they helped granddaddy build this. "See, right here I put a hole in the wrong place, so I had to put a peg in it and redrill over here." Or they might say, "The company cut this mortise in the wrong place, so we had to put extra pegs in here and here." It was a great family project.

TEAMWORK

Our Sunday school class one quarter was considering the teamwork aspect of marriage. We agreed on the first day that good teamwork required leadership, communication, commitment, understanding of individual roles, and subjugation of individual accomplishments for the common good. As part of a homework assignment, we were asked to consider what our team of husband and wife thought was a task that clearly required teamwork. For Linda and me, the choice was immediate and clear: raising children. On multiple occasions, one or the other of us had said, "Don't you dare die and leave me alone to . . ." For us, it was always ". . . raise all these children." Perhaps for others it would be ". . . run this business" or ". . . grow old without companionship," but for us, the focus has long been raising children. When I offered that the next Sunday, it generated a discussion.

"I agree," someone said, "and last week I realized I hadn't been supportive enough of my spouse in dealing with our teenage daughter. When we fixed that, our daughter was surprised we were on the same page."

"Us too," someone else added. "When we aren't on the same page, we find the children playing us against one another."

There were several comments that echoed these sentiments. Clearly we had found a common chord of understanding. But the comments unsettled me. In each case, the team was a father and mother. The opponents were the children. I have no difficulty understanding the dynamic; it is just one I don't like. I much prefer being on the same team as my children. I prefer the opponent, if you will, to be external. My distress in times of conflict with my children, mostly daughters as it happens, is that it disrupts our internal team. Our goals are different, our priorities are disordered, leadership is challenged, and communication often becomes clouded or one-sided or confrontational. The team becomes dysfunctional.

We were building a house. We were building it ourselves with the help of family and sometimes friends. Our children were participating in the project, some to a large extent, others with a more limited involvement, but all participated. I tried to photograph each of them as they worked with me because I think the teamwork was valuable. The documentation will be of interest to them and their children, and those who know us will be interested to see us working together. I don't find it remarkable that my children were willing to give of their time to be with us and work, but others do. On a number of occasions I have heard, "That is remarkable. If I tried to get my children to work with me on a project like that, the grief would make us all miserable. It would probably be impossible to get them to do it, and your children are smiling and seem to be enjoying themselves."

Certainly, we are not unique and not even the best example of involving our children in family projects. We know a couple of families whose father works at home and has involved the children in his work. Farm families do this typically and with excellent results, but many other kinds of family projects work as well. While we lived in Vermont, gardening, working with our draft horses, tapping maple trees, and animal husbandry were things we all shared, each with a vital part. The Family Chorale—our family's singing group, explained in a later chapter—was teamwork in the best sense and involved family outside our immediate family. Preparing for concerts and preparing for a recording session made us work hard together with a goal in mind. Even now, if I am asked to sing at church, I usually prefer to sing with one of the family members while Linda accompanies and helps with the music selection. We did background music for 45 minutes at two fundraisers for a local charity and involved all the available children in one role or another. My latest passion is our barbershop quartet in which I sing with Timo, Kenneth, and Ben. The girls were subjected to hours of practice when we got together for Thanksgiving this year. It isn't the concert that is the goal, although that is often fun. It isn't sitting on the porch of a completed home enjoying the view. It isn't eating the eggs, drinking the milk, or pouring the syrup on the pancakes, although all those are benefits. It is working together with people you love on a project worth doing. It is the teamwork.

If the only benefit of this were that you reap the immediate benefits (syrup, eggs, vegetables), it would be worth the effort. But the real benefits are far greater—a strong work ethic in the children, building rapport with them, molding and understanding their personalities, and building a relationship that has a good chance of surviving the stresses of the teen years. But greatest of all is ending a period of stewardship with the best of all possible outcomes, a godly young man or woman and a heavenly Father who says, "Well done, good and faithful servant" (Matt. 25:21). I pray I hear those words.

Can I do better as a father and husband? Without question. Linda could make a long list of ways (she doesn't, but I'm certain she could). Does our teamwork suffer because I am less than Christ-like? Yes (too often). Do I have issues in clear communication, and do I sometimes fail to listen carefully? Sure. There are always opportunities to improve. But I am grateful that at a time early enough to rescue it from the difficulty it was headed toward, God set my feet on a track to focus on my family and gave me the wisdom to develop a team named the Shermans.

THE POWER OF A NAME

My father told me a story that made an impact on me years after he told it. He was a college student far from home and knew no one there, but he had a plan. Walking across campus between classes, he noted on a number of occasions an attractive young lady coming the other way. He asked around and discovered her first name—Susan. The next time he passed her, he greeted her. "Hi, Susan," and then he continued on his way. When next they passed, he again greeted her. "Hi, Susan."

She replied, "Hi, Jim." Eventually they got beyond first names and had a real conversation. The rest of the story is not important, but there was an important lesson for me in the first part. By learning her name, my father assigned value to her. He made the effort to learn her name. He thought she was worth the effort. Worth denotes value. When she responded with his name, she assigned value to him as well. The effort of learning someone's name assigns value to them.

I was talking about this at dinner one night, and Kristin responded, "There is a custodian at work who talks to me every day. It isn't a long talk, but he says, 'Hi, Miss Kristin, are you having a good day? Anything I can do for you today?' I don't know his name."

I asked her, "What is the name of your boss?"

"Mr. Smith."

"What is the name of the person in human resources you go to for a change in your schedule?"

"Abigail."

"Why do you know their names?"

"I have to know their names; they are important in my job."

"Then the custodian isn't important enough to you to learn his name."

She looked unhappy. "That isn't right, and it isn't how I feel. Of course he is important."

"I have a suggestion for you," I said. "Tomorrow, find out his name—not from him—and then wait until he comes around. When he does, greet him with his name and tell me what happens."

The next night at the dinner table, Kristin said, "His name is Mr. Johnson. When I saw him, I said, 'Hi, Mr. Johnson, how are you today?' We didn't have a long conversation, but it was different. I could tell from his eyes and the inflection in his voice that he recognized I had made the effort to learn his name. There was a connection that hadn't been there before."

I was glad she learned the value of learning a name. I was especially glad she knew immediately that he was worth the effort.

MY CHILDREN'S MARRIAGES

By the time I was emotionally ready to get married, I was fully independent of my parents. Although their love and support were important to me, they had no role in my choice to marry Linda and did not expect to have any. Thankfully, I knew they liked Linda and approved of my decision to marry her. As I got further and further into fatherhood, however, I was influenced by the conservative, religious community around me, a community that certainly had adopted an expanded concept of patriarchy. That word can carry lots of meanings, but for me, it suggested that my role as a father carried many responsibilities and a fair amount of authority that could impact how my children were prepared for and approached their marriages.

During this time, I wrote an article called "Daughters and Marriage" for the journal *Patriarchy*. If you want to read it, you can find it online using the title and my name. I tried hard to accurately understand what I read in the Bible, primarily in the Old Testament, and to apply it to today's New Covenant culture. In doing so, I was influenced by someone who had developed a large ministry using principles developed from Old Testament stories and broadening their application. Over the subsequent years, I have understood the danger of this approach and write about it briefly in the essay "Truth, Evidence, and Decision-Making." The way I communicated in the *Patriarchy* article was dogmatic and legalistic, and while I still support much of what I said, if I wrote something like that today, I would write with considerably more humility and a softer tone. My three daughters and a daughter-in-law describe the article as harsh, legalistic, and rigid. However much truth there is in the article, by the time my daughters were approaching marriage, they had made it very clear that I was not going to be in charge of the process.

I wrote the article in the earlier years of my fatherhood before life rubbed off many of my rough edges, a process described by my daughter Rachel as a "real-life, hands-on experience with the challenges of raising daughters." She went on to say, "I came away with much appreciation for you and how you've challenged yourself and grown as a father throughout the years. It is important that I tell you the following: I am extremely grateful for the way you and Mom raised us. I understand there are things you might do differently now, having more experience, but you did the best you could in the moment, and you have raised three very well-adjusted daughters of whom, I believe, you are very proud. You raised us to be hardworking, to respect authority, and to understand and carefully manage our finances. You taught us that submission to a husband is important but that it should not ever come at the cost of abuse or harm. You taught us to have a strong belief system and fight for what we wanted in our lives."

What led to the change? I observed men taking rigid positions with their children and demanding complete authority without the humility of publicly recognizing their own sinfulness and fallibility. I saw them drive away their children to the point that reconciliation seemed impossible. I saw too much law and too little grace. I also saw the wounded spirits of my children when I wronged them and recognized my need to apologize and to change. I did not want to wrong them over and over in the same way; I wanted to learn from my mistakes and do better. I saw that raising my children was my responsibility because God put me in the position of steward, not owner, and that raising them correctly was to make them spiritually strong and great tools in His hands. I felt that responsibility equally for my sons and my daughters. If my daughters saw submission to a husband as their godly responsibility, they would submit from a position of strength, not because I had put them in a position of weakness from which they had no other choice. To help them become that kind of adult, they needed my guidance, discipline, and an abundance of love, acceptance, grace, empathy, and encouragement—precisely the same things I was so grateful to have received from God.

What does that have to do with marriage? Everything. If I did my job well, by the time they felt ready for marriage, my children would be spiritually mature and could make their own choices, follow them through, and succeed in their marriages. One child married the child of a family with whom we had worshiped for years. One married someone we hardly knew. Some married spiritually mature adults; two married someone recently saved. Each of my children discussed their plans with Linda and me. They requested guidance, and we gave them the best we could. On one occasion, we thought a marriage would be a mistake. We said so, and after a time, the marriage was called off, not because of our objections but because our child eventually saw those same things as problematic. Our sons and daughters have approached their marriages differently, sometimes dramatically so. Their marriages do not all follow the same script.

What I tried to do in the journal article referenced above was to set out the best pathway to marriage for my daughters. I could have written similarly for my sons. I still think there is a best way to approach marriage, and some of my children came pretty close to that ideal. Others chose another path, one often dictated by choices they had made earlier in life. The consequences of those choices made a new reality for them, a reality that then offered a different set of choices and another opportunity to make a best decision. Some children have heard me repeat to them, "I may hate the decisions you make, but there is nothing you can do that will make me quit loving you." In some of the essays that follow, there is a discussion of how this worked out. I have occasionally described my daughters as the anvil on which God hammered me. Ultimately, my children and I all learned lessons, maturity deepened, and love prevailed.

Timo setting floor joists

Chris using "come-along" to bring the joints together

Jim and Rachel. This rafter had to be removed. The rafters to either side needed to be installed first to stabilize the ridge beam.

Completed timber frame

Kristin and Dorothy handing up smaller rafters

Entry into Maple Ridge and sugar house

Maple Ridge from the other side of the valley. Sugar house and completed house can be seen

House at Maple Ridge

Nuclear family, 1996

Nuclear family, spouses, and grandchildren at Rachel's marriage to Chris Page, October 2019

COURTSHIP

Lots of parents in the United States, probably the great majority, stay pretty much out of their children's love lives, and for good reason. It is a minefield with multiple opportunities to make a mistake, with potentially serious consequences if you do so. But if parents don't help, is a mistake less likely? The marriage statistics, abortion rates, and rates of teen pregnancy would suggest otherwise, and those problems are certainly not limited to secular society. I was a fan of courtship, which for our family was defined as a relationship focused on deciding whether the one being courted was a potential spouse. Courtship was exclusive; you did not court more than one person at a time. Courtship went on to marriage, or it ended. Dating was more for fun, was not exclusive, and had no particular end in sight. I understand from my younger children that the definition of dating has changed, but it is still different than courting. Because there is no universally accepted definition of courtship, it can lead to misunderstanding and confusion. My older sons accepted my understanding.

The boys, to date, have been pretty easy. We discussed the difference between dating and courting. They thought courting was better, and there was never any particular conflict. At worst, a couple of times I had to remind them that they had some things to accomplish in their lives before they could enter into a courtship. But generally, I think Scott, Chris, Timo, and Kenneth (all married now) have made excellent decisions, and it all worked out pretty well. I cannot stress enough how different it has been with the girls, at least with Kristin and Dorothy.

But first, a word about Rachel. As tough as she was as a little girl, she was easy as a teen. She listened to me, she generally agreed with me, I have the feeling she loved and respected me, she problem-solved the same way I do, she was logical, she liked sports, she loved being tall, and she thought a relationship with a man was good but far in the future. Anything beyond a peck on the cheek she generally regarded as gross. While she was lovely and feminine, there was an aspect to her that said, "Keep your distance, or you're going to get hurt." That, combined with her height, kept her admirers (and she certainly had them) at a distance. Rachel married in 2019, after a courtship by the above definition, to a man who asked my permission before he asked her to marry him. The picture of our extended family on page 73 was taken at their wedding.

Part of the reason I wanted to move to Roanoke, Virginia, was that I felt my daughters needed to meet boys who didn't chew tobacco. We looked for a church with an active youth group, acknowledging there could be difficulties with that. After we found one, Timo became part of the leadership team for the group. I suspected that boys might be interested in Dorothy, as she was as cute as the dickens and very nice. Because she was cute and interested in being cute (she spent a lot of time on her appearance, more than I approved of, but I seemed powerless to affect the situation), I scheduled our courtship-giving-of-the-heart discussion earlier than later. We went to dinner. "Dorothy, you have seen the heart necklaces I've given your sisters."

"Yep," she replied.

"I know you understand, but just to make sure, let me review. If you take the heart and give me the key, you are agreeing that I have control. You are agreeing not to give your heart to anyone I have not given the key to. If someone is interested in you, you need to send them to me. If I give my approval, I will give them the key, although only you can decide if you give them your heart. It is my hope that you will keep your heart for the one you eventually marry."

"I do understand that, Daddy," she said.

75

"You don't have to make a decision tonight," I told her. "I want you to be sure this is what you want to do."

"It is," she said, "I'm ready to give you the key to keep for me." We bought her the heart, she gave me the key, and she wore the heart on a necklace we bought. Fast-forward a year or so.

"Dorothy, I think he is a very nice young man, but you and he are too young (14 years old) to have this kind of a relationship. You can be friends, but that's it. Cool your jets." I didn't get a whole lot of response. I also talked to the boy's mother (his father was out of town). "I don't want there to be any misunderstanding. I like your son just fine; he seems to be a terrific kid. And it may well be that he and Dorothy will be married someday. It's just that they are too young now. I have asked Dorothy to cool down the relationship, and you may hear about it."

"That's fine," she responded. "We don't believe in dating, either, and we've also been concerned about the amount of time they've been spending together."

Fast-forward two weeks. "Dorothy, I'm going to let you go on this overnight youth trip, particularly since Timo is going to chaperone. You need to make good decisions, and you know what I'm talking about."

"Yep, I will," was her only response.

It isn't that I thought Dorothy hated me, but I was clearly not her first choice of someone to spend a lot of time with. She could talk for hours on instant messenger or the phone with her friends, but I didn't get much. There didn't seem to be active rebellion, just no common interest.

Timo came to me on Sunday afternoon after the trip. "I caught Dorothy sitting on the boy's lap in the hot tub. I asked her if she was going to talk to you about it, and she said no. I talked to the boy, and I'm sure nothing else happened."

"What do you think I should do, Timo?" I asked. After all, he was a youth leader. Surely he would have wise counsel. Well, maybe not. I have never seen such a deer-in-the-headlights look from Timo. He immediately shook his head; no help from him.

Dorothy had gone to her room. I went outside and washed the car. I washed three cars. I finally decided what I wanted to do. I talked it over with Linda. "Oh," she exclaimed, "you'd better talk that over with his parents."

I called his dad and explained my problem and what I wanted to do. "Sounds okay to me," he said. "Let me talk to my wife." He called back in a couple of minutes. "Let's do it right after church tonight."

After church I went up to the young man and greeted him. "I want to talk to you and your dad." The boy seemed calm, certainly more so than I would have been at that age. We went into a back room where we could be alone. "What happened this weekend was done despite both sets of parents asking you and Dorothy to be friends and nothing more," I told him. I explained the heart ceremony and what it signified. "You and Dorothy have decided that you know more than your parents and have pursued a relationship we did not approve of. Dorothy has, without my permission, clearly given you her heart, and you have accepted it. I am smart enough to know when I am beaten. Here is the key." I pulled it out of my pocket and held it in my hand, not giving it to him quite yet. "I will give you the key since you already have her heart, and with it I give you, and her, my approval to pursue your relationship. If you take it, I will anticipate a period of courtship and engagement not longer than a year. You should plan on marriage within that period."

He did not reach for the key. He also didn't flinch, stammer, faint, pale, or run. He calmly said, "I don't think I am going to be ready for marriage within that time."

"Actually, I agree with you," I assured him. "And if you had foolishly thought you were ready, your father and I would have tried to convince you otherwise. But know this; if you are not ready for marriage, then you have no business with my daughter's heart. You do not have my permission to pursue it or the relationship."

"Can we be just friends?" he asked.

"You had that opportunity and blew it. If she escapes the controls I am about to put on her and approaches you, I suggest you run."

"Can I explain to her why I didn't take the key?" he requested.

"Yes, in the presence of Timo, me, or your father," I said. Timo was his choice.

I came away very impressed with this young man. Although I thought he and Dorothy had made a mistake in their relationship, I could see the quality in each of them that made them mutually attractive. I can be intimidating, and I was certainly not trying to be gentle. He did not appear intimidated at all. His first thought was for Dorothy and wanting her to understand. Dorothy, for her part, accepted her restrictions quite well. She was pulled out of youth group and attended adult Sunday school with me. She sat with me in church and wasn't allowed to go on any outings that might present difficulty. Eventually, she did talk to me and to her older sisters. If I had to guess, I would say she was in a situation she could not control on her own and, at some level, grateful for the control I established. Over time, she has earned back privileges. She may again make a mistake. But as important as it is to protect her, it is also important to respect her judgment, allow her to make a mistake and grow from it, and to forgive her when she acknowledges error. Lest you wonder, this is included with Dorothy's permission. This essay was written within a year after the events. There is more to tell that is included in the essay "Independence."

There will be those who read this and think I overreacted; others will think I am a poor father for having allowed my daughter to be put in that position at all. In some ways I agree with both perspectives. I am stuck with making the best decisions I can with the information and understanding I have at the time. Reading this may make you better prepared for your own challenges.

Kristin was a whole different ball game. During her alien abduction period, I found a letter addressed to a neighborhood boy.

(I wasn't snooping around; she left it in a public place, and I picked it up to put it away.) The letter was relatively innocuous but was signed, "With all my heart, all my love, forever yours." In the context of the heart ceremony described above, that was inappropriate. In addition, this was a young man who would never be appropriate for Kristin for a number of reasons, and this happened during a time when Kristin was in active warfare with me. I left a note on her pillow saying, "I found the attached letter. It is clear you don't want to honor the commitment you made to me. Here is the key; it doesn't do me or you any good for me to have it in these circumstances. Don't give it back to me unless you mean it."

I was told later that she cried uncontrollably when she found the note. Linda told me she had a number of conversations with her. Eventually, a couple of years later, she did give me back the key. I'm not much of a poet, but I wrote a poem after she gave it back to me.

She Gave Me the Key to Her Heart

She gave me the key to her heart
She had mine right from the start
Her hand on my arm
Her eyes soft and warm
So wonderful, God's work of art

One June I walked down the aisle
My face was wreathed in a smile
The girl of my dreams
As strange as it seems
Thought a life with me was worthwhile

My daughter has asked for my aid
For God's perfect match she has prayed
Her father she trusts

To weed out what rusts
Discover what never will fade

One day I will give back the key
For a man on whom both will agree
She'll give it to him
Heart filled to the brim
God's best, to the highest degree

She gave me the key to her heart
She had mine right from the start
Her hand on my arm
Her eyes soft and warm
So wonderful, God's work of art

INDEPENDENCE

If the goal of raising children is to have them become godly men and women who are ready and able to be effective witnesses of the power of Christ in their lives, then part of that package must be to help them develop independence from parental authority. While the goal is clear, the pathway to achieving that goal is often fuzzy.

To use an absurd illustration, I want my children to learn to drive safely; I certainly don't want to have to chauffeur them around when they are 35 years old. Do I then allow my two-year-old to drive the car on the interstate? Obviously not. That is too much independence at a time they are not ready for it. What is the right amount? When do you give it? How much oversight do you provide? Are they ready?

During adolescence, most children are more interested in gaining independence than their parents are in allowing it. Adolescents usually go through a period of magical thinking. If you ask them what would happen if a teen got drunk, stole a car, and tried to outrun the police down a dark mountain road, they would respond that it is likely to end very badly. If you ask them why they didn't think about that when they did it, they would say, "I didn't think it would happen to me." Magical thinking allows them to doubt that there will be unpleasant consequences to behavior they know would be unacceptable to their parents. Since some consequences to bad behavior can be permanent, life-altering, and life-ending, parents are reluctant to grant too much independence. But failure to grant independence stifles development and leads to either continued dependence or rebellion, a tension that makes parenting teens the most difficult job I have ever undertaken. I think teens need enough independence to make decisions even if there are bad consequences (hopefully not too bad) they have to work through. That is how they learn. I sometimes say, "Wisdom comes from experience; experience comes from lack of wisdom," and this applies to all ages and levels of maturity.

After graduating from high school, Scott took a job in a small construction company. He had a truck he had completely rebuilt. He worked hard, he was reliable, and he was a valued employee. He still lived at home, ate most of his meals there, and generally participated in family activities, and we were glad to have him there. My mindset was that he was now an adult, and I would treat him as such. I gave him pretty much complete freedom in setting his schedule, his finances, and more. And since he was an adult, I anticipated he would see things that needed doing and pitch in to accomplish them. I certainly would if I were living in someone's home. Scott didn't. If something needed doing, I did it or got one of the other kids to do it. On occasion, I would ask him to do something, and sometimes he did. I became increasingly frustrated because he was not meeting my expectations of adult behavior despite the fact I was treating him as one.

His mother had a different mindset. She saw this as a gradual process. If he had been accountable to her last week for his schedule, he still was this week. She wanted to know his plans, when he would be home, if he was going to be gone for the weekend, where he was going, with whom, and so on. On the other hand, she was still willing to do his laundry, cook his meals, and do his shopping. I think without ever really considering it, Scott took advantage of the best of both worlds. He got his mother to do stuff for him and claimed the independence I offered without taking on all the responsibilities. My frustration grew to the point that I wanted him out of the house.

Then I had a flash of insight. There is a principle of child-rearing that states this: children do not live up to your expectations; they live up to your inspections. You could add this: children cannot live up to either expectations or inspections if they don't know what they are. I had never sat down with Scott and talked through this new paradigm. I had never clearly laid out for him the expectations, and I had never explained how disappointed I was in his failure to live up to them. Scott, bless him, knew there was a problem but really didn't know what it was all about. Talking through it didn't make all the problems go away, but it set a basis for future communication. He had a clearer idea of what I expected; I had a basis for going to him if I thought his behavior did not meet the level I wanted. Linda and I talked about making sure she and I were giving the same message and operating on the same basis. Thereafter, things got better, and having him around got to be fun again.

Chris went directly to college after high school. He lived in an apartment behind our house but was still very involved in family life. Although he had wanted to be more involved in campus life right away, we lived too far from the college. At the beginning of his third year, he told us he was moving to an apartment near campus to live with friends. Because of his scholarships, there was no financial disincentive. Chris was mature beyond his years, so I had no concerns. Linda was devastated, seeing his move as a statement about the priority of family. We talked about it, Chris moved, Linda adjusted, and it made it easier for the next child. Sometimes two goods compete. Family is good. Independence is good. Participation in campus life is good. Going to church with your family is good. Being a part of worship with a campus Christian group is good. The goods competed, and Chris made a choice; it was his to make.

Kenneth did well his first year of college, entering at age 16½. However, he lost focus his second year and spent much more time on a computer game than on schoolwork. The fact that school was a higher priority than a game was not a mystery to him; this was no failure to communicate. When his grades came out, we had a discussion. "What are you planning to do, Kenneth?"

"I don't know. I really don't know what to major in."

"Then going on in school seems like a bad idea. What are you going to do instead?" I asked.

A couple of days later he told me he had enlisted in the army. Going in shortly after his 18th birthday, he chose infantry and air-borne as his enlistment options. He was in the invasion of Iraq and spent 12 months there. Had he been killed or seriously injured, I would have struggled with it, but even then I would have concluded that the decision not to allow him to continue in college was the right one. He needed to experience the consequences of his actions. As a result of what he went through, he became a serious student at Liberty University, is now married to a wonderful young woman, and is a mature, independent man. The army did what I could not do.

In the above examples, the children are sons and out of high school. The difficulty of transition from dependence to independence starts way before that time. Children become capable of independent decision-making in some areas while not being ready for others. In legal terms, this ability to be independent is called competence. Adults may be competent to drive a car and make decisions about their healthcare but be incompetent to sign a contract. In legal issues of competency, a judge may set a reasonable person standard, deciding a person is competent in a legal sense if they make decisions in a particular area as a reasonable person would do. If that seems a little arbitrary to you, it does to others as well. Interestingly, once judged competent, a person can make decisions that a reasonable person would *not* make, termed irrational decisions. For instance, given the health risks of cigarette smoking, a person who decides to continue to smoke might be considered to have made an irrational decision, but we allow competent persons to make that decision. Taken one step further, if you are a minor, you are not allowed to purchase cigarettes; you have no legal standing as competent to make that decision until you achieve the age of majority.

This has some interesting parallels in parenting. As a parent, I take the position as judge or legal counsel. The child is requesting limited competency. "Daddy, can I have an allowance and spend it how I want?" "Daddy, can I have a dog? I'll take care of it." "Daddy, I'm old enough for a driver's permit. Can I get one?" I have to decide if the child has achieved the level of maturity to make it likely they can avoid too much trouble if given this level of independence. I may anticipate that they will abuse the privilege and decide to maintain some level of supervision. Supervision will allow me to monitor the decision-making, protect them from a bad decision that has an unacceptable consequence, and use their mistakes to refine and improve their decision-making. If it all works well, there will be progressively more independence, a gradual learning process that leads to wisdom, and a maturing relationship as my child grows and develops into an adult. It is seldom that smooth, however. I don't have the requisite wisdom, the child doesn't want that much supervision, and there is often a disconnect between what I think and what they want.

One daughter wanted a lot more independence than I wanted to allow. She had a focus that was quite different than the one I wanted her to have, a focus that led her to make decisions I didn't like. I saw her actions as evidence that she needed less independence and more control. She saw my response as controlling and unreasonable, so she avoided my supervision. That gave her less parental consequence but made me feel she was untrustworthy. This process began around age 12, was pretty bad by age 14, and became unacceptable at 16. She was rebellious and escaped parental control at every opportunity. We tried everything we could think of, but the situation went from bad to worse. Finally, I took her out to dinner, and we talked about the situation. I knew she had considered leaving home (since she was not a competent adult, this would have been running away). I pointed out that she had little or no option for survival other than prostitution, whether to one man or many. I offered to relax my restrictions, allow her to work, do minimal school, save money, get her GED and a driver's license, and leave home at 17 with more options for self-reliance. In exchange, I asked if she could quit lying and sneaking out, communicate better, and participate in family activities. She agreed. On her 17th birthday, a young man from another state showed up at the house, and she drove away with him in a car I provided. We did not know she had developed an online romance with him. We knew his family but not much about him. She had not gotten her GED or driver's license because she refused to fill out the necessary paperwork. A week later, they were married in a justice of the peace ceremony with no family in attendance. I had to send a notarized statement that I was allowing her to marry.

During the years of conflict with a daughter I loved deeply, things were tough. I had many moments of absolute despair, crying into my pillow at night. Linda often comforted me, saying, "It'll be okay," and I responded, "I just can't see how it can possibly be okay." At other times, I did the comforting. Both of us were miserable about the situation. I felt like a failure. God had given me this child to nurture into a godly, mature adult, and she had left in rebellion to me and to God, immature, vulnerable, and in danger. I was absolutely frightened but saw no alternative. What happened, as detailed above, was an attempt to preserve the opportunity for a future.

I learned these things:

1. It was important for me to not create barriers for a future relationship. There will be many years, I hope, for my daughter and her family to have a relationship with us. There will be maturing and growth for both of us. Down the road, she will have built a life that is her own; I would like to be part of it. I tried hard to transmit a message that I did not approve of or like her decisions but valued her and loved her and wanted the best for her.

2. She is my daughter given by God. She is God's child first and foremost. Although I may be distressed at the direction she has taken, God knew this all along. If He is sovereign, and I believe He is, it is His hand that guides her and allows her decisions. My vision for her life was a figment of my imagination; God's vision for her life is a reality. She may reject my vision, but she will live out His vision and be His tool for His use.

3. I need to be sure my distress is not my pride. As people see the path she takes, they may conclude it is a reflection of my parenting. To a large extent, I agree. I am a flawed and sinful person, and that had to have had an impact on her. To balance that, my other children have taken different paths. Are those different, more acceptable paths also a reflection of my parenting? Yes, to about the same extent. I have tried to use the instructions in God's Word in my parenting; to the extent I have been able to do so, things have gone well. Neither this child nor my others are free of sin or error, just like their father. No child has a perfect earthly father; becoming a godly man or woman does not depend on the perfection of the parent but on the grace of God. If others in the church or elsewhere conclude I am a flawed and imperfect father from the traits they see in my child, the reality is that they are correct. Why should that bother me? If I have pride in myself, it is sorely misplaced anyway.

Years later, this daughter and her four children now live in our house. When she returned, she was desperate, failing to provide for herself or the children, without resources, without other acceptable options. She was able to return to us because we had consistently maintained contact, tried to be supportive without enabling, and let her know that we were available to help her. In the years she was gone, she saw her rebellion and decisions as sinful and asked forgiveness. Of course, she received it. We carefully avoided any communication that was anything but empathetic, loving, supportive, and uplifting. We tried hard to act toward her as we would hope Christ would act toward us when we fail. Our daughter swallowed her pride, admitted she needed help, and the prodigal child returned home to a warm welcome.

She has become a fantastic woman, wonderful mother, skillful professional, leader, and someone I am honored to call my daughter. I could not be more proud of her.

If I have learned anything about how to guide a child through the process of maturing and becoming independent, it is that the journey is different for each. The consistent message is to love, to listen, to be open, to be flexible as the situation demands it, and to keep the focus on the correct goal, on love, and on Christlike behavior.

When my daughter left, I tried to understand her perspective and write about it. I also tried to put into words what one of her sisters might have said to her. The sister, when she read it, cried, and agreed that it captured her feelings. The hope expressed in the last verse is now the reality. Thank you, Lord!

Oh, Daddy, please
Just let me be
Your law my spirit galls.
I cannot breathe
I want to flee
From rules, constraints, and walls.
I need to grow
And find, my way,
The lessons life will teach.
I don't need you
My way I'll pay
No limits on my reach.

INDEPENDENCE

Oh, sister, dear
I once thought thus
Rejecting Dad's advice.
I fought with him
And made a fuss
I made him pay the price.
But now I see
The evidence,
It hurts to play with fire.
I did not know
The consequence
Of unrestrained desire.

Oh, daughter mine
I love you dear
It hurts to let you go.
I want to hold
And keep you near
Protect you from the foe.
To hear your voice
And see your smile
And know you're safe and glad,
I'd run the race
The thousandth mile
To keep you from what's bad.

The walls you hate
The rules you fight
Were based on God's own will.
To prevent sin
And Satan's might
From coming in to fill.
Not mine, but His

Rejected law,
Your welfare our intent.
Unfortunate,
Your way He saw;
Down your own path you went.

Oh, daughter dear
With hope and prayer
We sent you on your way.
We trust that God
From Satan's lair
Deliverance has paid.
One day to find
You have returned
Unto God's sovereign might
His tool to use
Because you've learned
His laws are your delight.

UMBILICI

I was in the emergency room evaluating a child brought in for near drowning. Fortunately, by the time he got there, he was pretty much back to normal and alert—a little overwhelmed by the ambulance ride, but doing okay. I talked to his parents and the nurses and took a look at him. "What's this thing?" I asked him.

"My belly button," he assured me a little quizzically, probably thinking it wasn't much of a doctor who had to ask. (Well, maybe not. He was only three and probably didn't think very abstractly. Maybe he was just proud he knew.)

"What does it do?" I asked further. He didn't say anything. "You have eyes for seeing and ears for hearing. What does a belly button do?" Still no answer. "Do you want to know?" I asked. "Since I'm a doctor I know these things." He nodded. The nurses leaned in; his mother attended. I guess they had been wondering what it was for, too. "God put it here for your daddy," I assured him. "When your daddy's fingers get cold, he can stick them in to get them warm." The nurse giggled, and the boy wasn't sure he believed me; his mom thought that was probably right.

In fact, the umbilicus (umbilici is the plural) is well-known in the Sherman family to be the property right of the father. The children are mostly in charge of their own bodies, and when they are tickled to the point that they need relief, they can proclaim, "Please, stop," and the tickling must immediately stop. Snuzzling necks and sloppy kisses are similarly under some semblance of the subject's control (though complete honesty would compel me to admit an occasional delay in complying with the command). The belly button is the one part of the child's body that is completely the father's. We know them as "Daddy's belly button on Dorothy's belly," for instance. Linda, having had a childhood deprived of such important information, seemed to have trouble comprehending this. In particular, she had trouble accepting the well-known fact that upon marriage, the rights to the belly button immediately are transferred to the husband. Further, she somehow got the idea that similar rights passed to the wife, a ridiculous concept as I'm sure you, dear reader, will agree.

Anyhow, one day I got an unexpected letter. It seems that after a mildly rowdy episode between Linda and me in bed one night, during which I had to go to great lengths to protect from violation my father's belly button on my belly, Linda called my father—in the Philippines! To my utter dismay and astonishment, he took her side in this dispute. Betrayed by my own father! He had written out a legal document transferring all rights to the belly button on my belly to Linda. I was aghast. I still can hardly believe it. Linda still has the title and brings it out at particularly difficult times.

Our family has developed a tradition of doing a humorous skit and singing a song at our children's wedding rehearsal dinners. At the rehearsal dinner the night before Timo's wedding, Scott, Chris, and Kenneth did a *VeggieTales* Silly Songs with Larry song called "Belly Button" by the Boyz in the Sink. They changed the words only a little. I then presented Rachel, his bride-to-be, with the title to his belly button. The ceremony was a big hit. Timo didn't object at all; I think he was looking forward to her claiming her rights.

CHARGE TO THE GROOM

At Timo and Chay's reception, I was asked to give the charge to the groom. I don't remember doing that for Scott's or Chris's wedding; I'll have to ask Linda if I did.

Timo married Rachel. Her first and middle names are Rachel Marie, and I have a biological daughter named Rachel Marie Sherman. Since Timo's wife took his last name and we all lived in the same city for a while, it got very confusing. Thus, his Rachel was Chay, and my biological daughter became LiLi. Timo and Chay were married on the shore of Lake Superior, a very long way from Florida. Scott and Tracy went to Timo's wedding from New Orleans. Since Tracy was quite pregnant at the time and their children, Aaron and Nathan, were young, the ride looked daunting. I met them in Nashville, and we took a couple of days to travel up to Wisconsin. At this time, I had not been able to spend much time with Aaron or Nathan, and they were not altogether sure who I was. On previous visits, I had noted that Scott was playing games with Aaron that I had invented and played with my children. Scott had learned them from me. All of this is to explain the following charge to the groom:

> I met Scott and Chris and their families in Nashville and traveled up with them. On the trip, I had some time to get reacquainted with Aaron, who has grown up quite a bit since the last time I saw him. He has become very verbal and interactive. I'm a pediatrician; I like children. In addition, I've been excited to have grandchildren and want a relationship with them. So I picked up Aaron and put him on my lap.

He wasn't altogether sure about that, but he put up with it. Then I laid him on my lap and flipped him, feet over head so he landed on the ground. He looked at me with indignation and said, "Don't do that; it's my daddy's."

"Well," I defended myself, "who do you think taught that to your daddy?" The logic of this was completely lost on the four-year-old. I tried to play a tickle game, one I had used with great success on my own children. "No!" was his vigorous response. "That's my daddy's!" This was an outcome I had never anticipated. I can't play my games with my grandson because my son, who learned them from me, has made them his own. I am both gladdened and disheartened (but mostly gladdened).

What does this have to do with a charge to the groom? Lots. Just as Scott has learned games and styles of interacting with his children from me, so you, Timothy, have observed years of interaction between your mother and me. There will be things you know you want to do better and other things you take for granted. But let me tell you that if you copy my interaction with your mother, you will have set your standard far too low because there is a standard that is much better, and that is the one you need to know and copy. That standard you can see in Ephesians 5:25, beginning with the words, "Husbands, love your wives, as Christ loved the church." Timothy, my greatest desire is that you take the things you have learned from me, separate the good from the bad, and build on the good and teach that to your children, that you and I may have a godly influence on the land and be fit instruments in the hand of God. That, Timothy, is my charge to you. God wants you to love Rachel with the same passion and dedication He gave us. And he gave *everything* for us. That is your standard.

LESSONS

"Daddy, I want to ride a bike around town with the other kids," Dorothy announced to me. We were living in McIntosh, there were plenty of neighborhood children, the streets were safe, people watched out for one another, and she would be with older brothers and sisters. It seemed reasonable, but there was just one problem.

"You don't know how to ride a bike," I pointed out.

"Buy me one, and teach me," she responded.

A couple of days later I came home with an appropriately sized bike. "Here you go," I said.

"It doesn't have any training wheels," she protested.

"Nope," I agreed. "If you are going to ride around town, you have to be able to ride without training wheels. I really don't have time to teach you; you're going to have to do this on your own. You are not allowed on that bike out of our yard until you show me you can ride." We had a fairly long driveway with a gentle slope, a perfect place to learn to ride.

Three days later, Dorothy said, "Daddy, I can ride now. Can I go outside the yard?" She had taught herself. The only thing I had to do was provide the necessary ingredients.

Contrast that with the time I spent teaching Scott to ride. It took many sessions spread out over weeks. The biggest difference, in retrospect, was motivation. I wanted Scott to be able to ride. Other kids his age were riding, and by golly, my kid was certainly as athletic and gifted as any of them. It wasn't that Scott didn't want to ride, but he certainly wasn't as motivated and focused as Dorothy. She practiced for hours on the driveway; he rode when I got out the bike.

Some things, I think, need to be taught, even if kids object. Swimming is an example. We have often lived near bodies of water and have had swimming pools. The night after we installed an aboveground pool at our house in Lutz, Linda and I hardly slept, thinking of a child drowning in it, so I built a deck with a locking gate that blocked the steps. Kenneth, then three years old, proudly showed me one day how he could squeeze around it and get up on the deck. None of my children were particularly enthusiastic about learning to swim, and I could empathize. My father taught me to swim, and I still remember the lessons and how much I didn't like them. Reason had little to do with it; I just didn't want to put my face in, I didn't want him to take me into deep water, and I certainly didn't want him to let go of me. But swimming became something I enjoy and do well, and I am grateful that Dad persisted and taught me. Eventually, I became a Red Cross lifeguard and water safety instructor and gave swimming lessons to hundreds of children one summer. Given our proximity to water, swimming seemed a necessity for our children, and I was the man to teach them.

During my fellowship training in Cleveland, I had little opportunity for swimming. One summer, however, we had a two-week vacation in Bradenton, Florida, near our families. Scott was four, Chris was two, and we spent the two weeks in an apartment complex with a pool. My brother Mike was renting the place and was out of town, and it was perfect for swimming lessons. We went down to the pool first thing in the morning, usually around 9:00 a.m., and had our lesson. Scott and Chris were not thrilled, probably for reasons very similar to mine at that age. I worked with Scott for a little while, then Chris, then Scott. We did a number of drills involving pulling with our arms, kick-kicking with our feet, blowing bubbles with our faces in the water, holding our breath under the water, and pushing off Daddy and gliding to the steps. Scott did okay; Chris loudly objected to pretty much everything. In fact, the first thing we heard in the morning, usually as the sun made its first appearance in the sky, was this: "We don't want to swim today." Actually, what they didn't want was a lesson; they loved the pool once the lesson was over.

We had an audience at the pool. Two elderly ladies were always there when we arrived and still there when we left. I think we intruded on what had previously been a peaceful, tranquil routine. They never said anything to me; I could sense the disapproval radiating from them. I imagined them thinking, "What an awful man. He is terrorizing those lovely children. They will probably be emotionally scarred for life." I kept a close eye out for child protective services.

We didn't seem to be making much progress with Chris, although Scott was beginning to swim by himself. The day before we left, though, something clicked. Chris suddenly quit protesting, jumped into the pool, and swam to me. He was beside himself. "Daddy, look at me." "Daddy, watch me jump in." "Daddy, come here so I can swim to you." "Daddy, watch me jump off the board." "Daddy, I can swim all the way across all by myself." He was in frenzied motion, so excited he could hardly talk, so full of accomplishment it oozed out of every pore. It was infectious. I know it was infectious because the old ladies caught it.

"Oh!" they exclaimed. "This is just so wonderful!" they gushed. "We have been here for the whole process and seen the whole thing. It's so wonderful that he has learned to swim. We are so excited for him." I had gone from the devil incarnate to a leading candidate for father of the year. I was safe from CPS.

I still don't know where the balance is, when it is fine to let kids direct the pace and direction of their learning and when I need to intervene. I think it varies with the issue; they don't get to choose whether to study science, but I am certainly in no particular hurry to teach them to drive. Also, it has become apparent to me that I am really not the best person to teach them some things.

For instance, consider the issue of keeping your room (and the house) clean. I have tried a number of innovative approaches to encourage the family to put things away. In this regard, at least, I acknowledge utter failure. Not one of my children cared in the least for a neat and tidy house, much less bedroom. For a time, I designated a big box as the destination for anything left lying around. If it didn't get put away, it got deposited into the box, and it stayed there until Friday when there was a public unpacking of the box with severe consequences to the individual who won by having the most articles. It worked—somewhat—but became me against them. If I came in the door, took off my gloves, put them on a chair, hung up my jacket, and turned around for the gloves, they were already in the box. The house did stay neater, but as soon as the box disappeared, so did the neatness.

Timo and Kenneth were both in college and living in a mother-in-law apartment next to our house. I once gave them an eviction notice for extreme slovenliness but relented when they admitted their error and promised to try to improve. Notice the word *try*. I don't know how hard they tried, but improvement was not particularly apparent. When Timo bought a house and lived there for some months prior to his marriage, his bedroom had a path from the door to the bathroom that was knee-high in clothes, trash, and sports gear. When he got married, however, almost immediately his house was as neat as a pin. I am told he takes off his clothes and puts them away. It just took the proper motivation, I guess; I'm not sure the motivation Rachel used would have worked for me. Timo isn't the only child who transformed once away from me; most of them are now much neater than when they lived with me.

Early in fatherhood, I had pretty firm ideas of what was right, appropriate, necessary, important, and useful. Sometimes those things were clearly godly as well, although I now think a lot of them were mostly my ideas of how I wanted my family to function. Now, many years later, I see them somewhat differently, viewing them through the eyes of my children who are now raising their families and trying to teach their children what they feel is important. The choices they make are not always the same as those I made. Is that because they see my choices as flawed? Is it because their spouses see things differently? Is it just that their priorities are different? I don't know; maybe it's all of these. They are all pretty terrific adults who have made their own decisions, some very unlike how they were raised, but it's nice to see that some of the lessons have stuck.

A STATE OF DISTRACTION

One day at work, a nurse asked me, "Is your son excited about going to Maryland?"

I was puzzled. Scott had attended the University of Maryland, but she didn't know Scott. He was now 32 years old, and I didn't know of any plans he had to return. She continued, "Katie is looking forward to the trip very much."

Katie is the same age as Ben, and I made the connection. The youth from church were going on a youth trip. Katie and Ben were in the youth group, and I had signed permission for Ben to go. The retreat must be in Maryland.

"Oh," I responded, "I guess so; I hadn't realized it was in Maryland."

While I was charting, she called her daughter. "Katie, have a good time. Make sure you pay attention to Pete (the youth minister). Did Dad give you money?"

I finished writing my note and called home. Ben answered. "Hey, Ben, are you ready to go?" Not quite yet; still packing.

"Do you have any pocket money?" Some, left from a birthday gift.

"Tell Mommy to give you $10 so you have enough. Have a good time; I'll see you in a couple of days."

About 15 minutes later, I got a call from Linda.

"The girls are so impressed," she said. "They couldn't believe you remembered and were so thoughtful to call and make sure Ben had enough money. Dorothy asked if I had reminded you. Kristin figured Ben or I had emailed you. They were astounded."

Why would they be astounded? Frankly, it was because the behavior was so uncharacteristic of me—not uncharacteristic that I would say goodbye, not uncharacteristic that I would want him to have some money, but very uncharacteristic that I would remember he was leaving and think to call and check that he had all he needed. That is a pretty sad but accurate commentary on me. I generally am, to say the least, distracted. At work I keep lots of things in my head and let few things drop. At home, I depend on Linda to keep me up-to-date. If she doesn't remind me, it isn't in my head. My forgetfulness is legendary.

One day on vacation, visiting a family we did not know at all well, I was sitting at a table with them, Linda, and the kids when it came up that it was Linda's birthday. I hadn't a clue. Actually, we were married for years before I could even tell you the date, and I am often not that sure. I could only come up with a couple of the children's birthdays but probably could tell you the months, if pressed. I showed up for a party once on the correct day but the wrong week. It isn't advanced age; I've always been that way. If you want me to remember something like that, a reminder the day before and another that morning is useful. For Linda, it has been a trial. Remembering birthdays is important to her. She is very forgiving, and I have given her lots of opportunities to demonstrate her charity. She didn't say so, but she was probably as surprised at my call to Ben as were the girls and probably hopeful I had begun a new period in my life, one of consideration and careful attention to detail.

I suppose I could have let her and the girls continue to think so. But they might have expected continued gentleness and thoughtfulness, and divine providence can only be pushed so far. I told Linda how it had happened. She laughed and laughed, mostly from the difference between what the girls had thought and the reality, but maybe due to relief that I was still the lovable, distracted man she knew so well.

TRUTH, EVIDENCE, AND DECISION-MAKING

I am a doctor and a pediatrician. I believe in an approach to health that includes healthy lifestyles and the best preventative medicine, including immunizations. I am also a man of faith and belong to a faith community that includes many people who have a different approach to health, particularly regarding immunizations. That has led to lots of discussions within my extended family and my faith community. This essay was written to explain my perspective and some facts I thought those people needed to hear. My children were brought up with these perspectives, but they often marry into families with other thoughts. I wrote this to help them gain insight into why I felt so strongly about the importance of correctly distinguishing truth, evidence, and expert opinion when they made important decisions. When I sent it to them, I got one response, one I did not expect. It is included at the end of this essay.

Decision-making is part of daily life. The decisions are sometimes trivial (what tie should I wear?) and sometimes very important (should I ask her to marry me?). It would be nice to have some assurance that our decisions are right. In medicine, the decisions a physician makes are often profoundly important to someone else—the patients—and a good physician wants to make the best decisions possible. In the last 20 years or so, an approach to problems has gained widespread acceptance as an approach that will lead to hopefully the best decisions. It is called evidence-based medicine.

The tenet is that where there is good evidence available, following it will benefit the most patients. The best level of evidence is the agreement of multiple, well-designed, randomized, controlled trials. Such trials try to remove any bias or chance and look at how some randomly assigned treatment will affect the carefully defined outcome. If many similar trials come to the same conclusion, then the statistical strength of a recommendation based on that evidence can be tremendous and much stronger than recommendations based on less-powerful evidence. Granting agencies like the National Institutes of Health are much more likely to give research support to the development of this kind of evidence, and there are more and more trials being done and reported. In the course of this research, we have discovered that the recommendations based on less-powerful kinds of evidence have been wrong. Expert opinion, usually based on the experience of physicians recognized by others in medicine as experts, has a dismal record. Unfortunately, expert opinion is still sometimes the best we have.

As good as it is, the best evidence in medicine is still not truth. Medical research yields statistics that may state that the chance that this conclusion is in error is less than one in 10,000. That would be strong evidence, indeed. Studies are considered statistically significant if the chance of error is less than 5 in 100. But whether it is 5 in 100 or 1 in 10,000, there remains a chance that the study is in error. Truth holds no chance of error. Truth may be misunderstood or misapplied, but truth is truth—it is never wrong. Unfortunately, there is no truth in statistics; it is too high a standard for medicine. Often we cannot find truth to apply to our daily decision-making, but truth does exist, and we can access it.

I accepted Christ as my Savior in my early 30s. I was already married, the father of two children, and fairly advanced in my training as a physician scientist. I had an intellectual conversion and a somewhat logical approach to my relationship with God. I accepted that God (in His three persons) was and is all-powerful, all-knowing, and simultaneously present throughout His creation (omnipotent, omniscient, omnipresent). I also accepted that the Bible represented His message to His people and that to the extent we could understand and apply it, we would honor Him, we would be closer to the center of His will, and the consequences of our actions would be less correction and chastisement and more blessing as we carried out His ultimate will. Recognizing that the Bible I read is a translation and that it contains both literal and figurative passages, and that complete and correct understanding is not within my capabilities, it still represents truth that I need to apply to my life. I started studying it and considering how it needed to impact all aspects of my life. In that decision and application, I had, and have, many companions. But our application of this principle of allowing God to inform and direct our lives has taken very different paths, sometimes in really opposite directions. Why? How can different people, sincerely studying the Word of God, end up with such different conclusions with such different impacts on their lives?

Our understanding of God's direction is colored by our under-standing, our prejudices, our circumstances, our culture, and our communities. They influence much about how we think. While we can know they are operant, it is very hard to come to scripture without letting these influences affect us. A good dose of humility is needed when we think about our ability to clearly understand many aspects of God's message.

Some traps seem worth mentioning. I discussed the problem with expert opinion in medicine, but it is an even bigger problem in religion. We are a people of faith. The object of that faith is God, but faith often spills over to a religious expert. The expert may be a pastor, an author, a deacon, or an invited speaker. They are likely to be sincere and convinced of the truth of their message. But they, like you and like me, are simply people. They may claim to be the spokespersons of God, but the Bible actually warns us about wolves in sheep's clothing. It might be that their insight is correct, or it might be wrong, but it is not truth unless it is precisely what God revealed in His Word—nothing more and nothing less. If the expert proclaims the necessity of accepting Christ as our personal Savior and leading our children to do the same, I will accept that as truth because the Bible clearly supports it. If their message is that vaccines are dangerous to our children or that female children should not attend college or that God loves white people more than people of other backgrounds, they are taking passages and extending their meaning and impact far beyond what the Bible clearly teaches. I have much experience personally and with friends and family who have been influenced by so-called experts. I cannot either prove or disprove the validity of the expert's message; I simply say it cannot be called truth. In my life, I might have been influenced by a message if it made sense to me, but it always had an asterisk by it in my mind. Be very careful of the advice of people who take a passage from the Bible, develop it into a principle, and extend it into many aspects of life.

Probably the least reliable expert is referenced by those who state, "I know this is true because I saw it on the internet." Unfortunately, I have often heard that from my patients.

Another way some Christians try to find truth is to put out a fleece. The fact that it worked for Gideon does not mean it will work for us. If we simply cannot come to a decision, even after prayer, discussion with our spouses and other loved ones, and careful consideration, maybe we should put the decision off for a while. If that is not possible, make a decision, trusting in God's grace and direction. He is sovereign, and He can bless a decision made by someone who is considerate and wants to honor Him. In other essays, I have discussed difficult decisions I made, particularly moving to Vermont and then moving to Gainesville, Florida. I cannot say whether the decisions I made were right. But I can confidently say that God blessed my family through both of them.

We want our lives to be governed by truth. Sometimes, evidence is all we have, sometimes not even that. God has given us the truth we most need. He has no illusions about our lack of perfection. He left us wiggle room. He wants us to remain true to Him. He wants us to allow Him to light our next steps, if not the entire path of the journey. He wants to bless us. I recommend the book *Decision Making and the Will of God* by Gary Friesen if you want a long, very biblical, very readable discussion of this topic.

I'll include one response to this essay below with the author's (my daughter's, as will become clear) permission.

From Kristin:

Hi, Dad!

I'm very glad that you wrote this essay! Your dedication to always seeking out biblical truth has been a huge impact in my life. Growing up, I mostly read love stories, and they led me to believe that there was only one true love for each person. It seemed that I had to randomly, almost magically, come across that one person who was my soul mate. It was very overwhelming and discouraging to think of the billions of people I had to sift through in order to find the one who would make my life complete. I remember having a discussion with you when Mike and I were dating, when you told me that my line of thinking was simply wrong. I remember coming away from that conversation knowing that there were definitely men who were *not* right for me, but it was very possible that there was more than one man who would make a perfectly good husband. At that time, I didn't like that either because I didn't want the responsibility of such a huge decision. I remember you telling me that God had given me scripture to weigh what a godly man should look like, and these were the qualities that are non-negotiable. But after that, there was choice. I needed to pray and seek council from those in my life who had wisdom and could provide input (you and Mom), but ultimately, I had to make a decision and then had to choose to live with it no matter what.

When we had this conversation, it was at a time that I wasn't sure if I should marry Mike or if I would even want to. I didn't know how to process through something that was not specifically stated in God's Word. You and Mom weren't telling me, "Yes, he is absolutely the one you should marry! We love him, and your life is going to be awesome as his wife." (Again, I was looking to not have the responsibility of my decision.) You told me that I had to weigh the nonnegotiables against scripture. I did, and Mike passed. I needed to look at his qualities and decide if those were the things that I wanted as a foundation in our marriage. After that, I had to look at his flaws and decide if I could live with them (marrying him under the assumption I could change him was not an option). I had to make a choice in a very gray area and then trust God to work His will through the decision that I made.

Looking back at that choice, I am confident that I made the right one. Not because my marriage has been without struggle and not because I gained any magical perspective that Mike is the perfect one for me, but because I see God's hand working through the decision I made. I prayed, I sought council, and then I put a stake in the ground on the choice I made with 100 percent commitment to see it through. I believe that because I desired to make a decision that honored you and Mom as my parents (which is biblical truth), I had the desire to be aligned with God's will for my life (also biblical truth). The decision I made was right for me, not because of the decision in and of itself but because my heart's desire was right before God.

Thank you for guiding me through that decision and giving me the power and mindset to navigate life's many gray areas.

HUNKS

Browsing through the sports section of a magazine one day, I happened upon the picture of the opening ceremony of the sumo wrestling season in Japan. They are some really big guys. I began to smile and then chuckle as I hatched a nefarious plan. After asking for permission to cut out the picture, I composed the poem that follows. I put the picture under the poem so Kristin would read the poem first, and then I set them on her pillow.

Ode to Hunkitudinance

My father, help me find.
A man with hunkitudinance
My wedding day with him I'll dance
A waltz or other kind

A hunk is all that I desire
No shrimp or flimsy man
A man with muscles lights my fire
My passions he does fan

A gentle man who loves me dear
Who cherishes my soul
One who provides and pats my rear
My welfare is his goal

To such a one I'll pledge myself
My all I'll give him now
It matters not if Japanese
A hunk will have my vow

Dorothy and Rachel found the pages first. Dorothy said, "That's just wrong."

Rachel howled, "Dad!"

Linda was quietly amused but didn't like the line about getting patted on the rear; I'm not sure why. (She seems to enjoy it when I do it. I think it was just that putting it down on paper was too public.)

I stayed up that night in breathless anticipation until Kristin got home from working at Olive Garden. I heard nothing. Still I waited. Then she came into the room, looking serious. She sat down next to me, took my hand in hers, and, looking deep into my eyes, said, "Daddy, we need to have a little talk about the definition of hunk."

It was sometime in her 13th year that Kristin was abducted by aliens. I didn't realize it at first, as the aliens who took her away had left one of their own in her place, a perfect physical double. But it certainly didn't act like her. My daughter, almost overnight, became confrontational, challenged the values she had previously accepted, was disobedient, and generally made it hard to interact with her in any pleasant way. I clearly felt this more than Linda did. I remember coming home from work one day and sitting in the car for a time. I wondered if there wasn't something left to be done at work because the prospect of going into the house was less pleasant than going back to work. Shortly, I opened my eyes (I had closed them as I mused the circumstances of life) to a knock at the window of the car. Linda was there to deliver a message. "Kristin says to tell you it's okay if you come inside the house."

Two years later, the alien and Kristin again switched, and I was delighted to have my wonderful daughter back. You often appreciate something more when you have lost it, and my relationship with Kristin was something I had taken for granted. I had made the assumption that my children would respond to the love, teaching, and care we gave them and simply accept the values we held dear. What happened with Kristin opened my eyes to a different possibility, one that frightened me. When eventually she decided that God and family were important to her, as they were to us, it was a blessing and a joy, and we developed a new relationship. Letting her know how much I love her is important to me, and writing a poem about hunkitudinance is one way I showed her.

EATING

Kenneth was courting a young woman from Lakeland, Florida. She still lived at home, and he had visited her a number of times and developed a relationship with her family. Since the relationship seemed to be progressing well, we decided our families should meet, and we invited Katie and her parents to spend Labor Day weekend with us in Roanoke. We found many things in common, including stories about scrambled eggs. It turned out that Katie and her father had a go-round with eggs that paralleled an interaction I had gone through with Kristin.

Kristin was about a year old and generally pretty easy. She was, at that time, sitting in a high chair and eating table foods. I don't remember being aware that she had particular likes and dislikes, not that it would have made much difference. Linda had fixed scrambled eggs for breakfast, and eventually I noticed Kristin wasn't eating hers, so I fed her—at least I tried to feed her. She initially seemed to take a little, although she didn't swallow them, and then she wouldn't take any more. I persisted; she refused. I insisted; she resisted. Linda left the table and went to the bedroom. Scott, Chris, Timo, and Kenneth retreated upstairs. More eggs got stuffed in, probably with some fatherly assistance. Kristin would have spit them out if my hand hadn't been in the way. Eventually she swallowed, and more went in. It was messy, and it certainly wasn't much fun. Some of the eggs got smeared around the environment, but most went where I wanted them to go. By the time it was over, the whole family was pretty traumatized. We cleaned up and went on with life, although without scrambled eggs for a very long time. About six months later, Linda served scrambled eggs again. There was tension in the air as everyone waited to see what would happen. Kristin looked at her plate. She looked at me. She looked at her plate again. She picked up her fork and ate her eggs. To say I was relieved would be an understatement. So why did I make such a big deal about it? You can certainly get through life without eating scrambled eggs.

I grew up in a family with strong eating preferences. One brother in particular was very picky, and my mother ended up making three recipes of some dishes to accommodate her children's requirements. Linda was exposed to some of this early in our marriage, and one of the few things we discussed about child-rearing (before the issue was staring us in the face) was that we would not fall into that trap. The rule became that you ate what was before you without saying anything about it. You didn't have to have more unless you complained, in which case you did get more. You could ask for seconds of what you wanted but only after you ate what was already served you. If you served yourself, you didn't have to take much of something, but you had to take some. We consistently applied this approach with all the children, and they ate pretty much everything. Since Linda had to make only one recipe, dinner time was not focused on making them eat their food—they just did. We liked it that way and felt good about the success of this particular parenting skill.

A cherished rule of parenting I have consistently applied is that a parent doesn't have to fight with his or her children about an issue but may just choose to ignore it, and I frequently do so. But if the parent decides an issue is worth fighting over, he or she should never, *never* lose. Children should learn at an early age that once they truly join the battle, they never win. Children, in my opinion, don't really want to fight, but they do want to win. Faced with the inevitability of loss, they will quit fighting. If this lesson is learned early in life, it makes parenting a lot easier.

So that is the context. We wanted our children to eat what was before them, and it was an issue worth fighting over. Just about everyone present at the scrambled egg event remembers it well, evidence of the trauma it inflicted on us all. Only time will tell if the children decide this is a rule worth carrying on in their homes.

Some years later, we were at a buffet restaurant, and I was helping Timo, about five years old at the time, load his plate. I added an olive at the end. He said, "Dad, I don't like olives." I added another olive. We sat down, prayed, and began eating, but he didn't seem to be eating the olive. I reached over, picked it up, and offered it. Obediently, he opened his mouth and took it. It stayed in for about three milliseconds before everything he had eaten came up and landed in his plate. After we cleaned the mess up, he got more food, although I made a command decision that I had adequately won and didn't add another olive. In fact, almost 20 years later, I don't think he's eaten another olive.

Kenneth has had his food stories, too. One day I was stretched out at the table with my feet far under it when I felt something hit my toe. It didn't really register until I felt it a third or fourth time. I looked and found a small collection of green pepper pieces Kenneth was surreptitiously tossing under the table. It was so funny that I let him get away with it.

At a church picnic in Florida, I was standing with some of the men around a tub of fresh oysters, shucking and eating. Scott came up to ask some question or another, and while he was there, I offered him an oyster. He preferred none. I insisted. He ate. I offered another, which he politely declined, and I did not insist further. He had tried one without any significant protest, so he was done. I thought no more of it. About five minutes later, Chris arrived. "Yeah, Dad?" he said with a questioning tone.

"What do you mean, 'yeah, Dad?'" I asked.

"Scott told me you wanted to see me."

I immediately understood. (I leave it for you to decide Scott's motive.)

"You need to eat one of these," I said.

He looked disgusted, opened his mouth, and ate it. "That's it," I said, and off he went.

Scott was having dinner with us one night after having not lived at home for some time. Linda had, in recognition of the occasion, made something unusual (we usually referred to this as one of Mommy's experiments). Scott took one taste and declared it gross. If you refer back to the eating rules above, you will see that such behavior was prohibited, and for good reason. Ben and Dorothy promptly decided that if their older and wiser brother thought it was gross, it clearly would be seriously poisonous. In very clear terms and with some emphasis and volume, I pointed out that Scott was responsible for this breach of table etiquette and responsible for what would now happen. I immediately gave Dorothy and Ben more of the offending substance. Scott quietly took the spoon, helped himself to more, and ate it without further comment.

Honesty and the fact that all my children will read this necessitate full disclosure. I would really prefer not to eat tofu or mushrooms. Mushrooms in particular just seem disgusting to me, overly dead in some way. When served mushrooms, I eat them without complaint, but I have to admit that Linda will cook meals with and without mushrooms. I also admit I have infected most, though not all, of my children with this dislike. Tofu, on the other hand, they all seem to tolerate. I generally discover I have had tofu sneaked into a meal when I go for seconds, and they all start giggling. I have gotten pretty suspicious about things that look like stews and casseroles.

One year, the pediatric residents in our program asked me to give them a talk about child-rearing and discipline. Since many of the residents come from much more liberal backgrounds, I wasn't sure that was a really good idea. They are smart, successful, generally very well adjusted, and know how they were raised (usually very differently than my children). But I gave the conference, and as an illustration of the principle of not losing a battle, I told the egg story. One of the first-year residents at the time later became a fourth-year chief resident and a very special friend of mine. As she was organizing conferences in her chief year, she confessed to me that she remembered that conference, but if I ever gave it again, I should definitely leave out the egg story.

I add this comment about 15 years after I wrote this essay. My children are now all adults, and most of them have children—I currently have 19 grandchildren. I noted above that only time would tell whether my children would adopt this approach with their children. I can say with absolute certainty that none of them have. While I prefer to think their spouses, raised in families with different rules, influenced that decision, I haven't asked.

RACHEL AND BASKETBALL

One night after work, I asked Rachel if she wanted to go shoot some hoops. We had been working that summer on playing in the post, on spin moves to the right and left, and on shooting from the free throw line and closer. Since she was 6 feet 2 inches tall at 15 years old, I thought she might have a future as a forward or center in college and certainly could get good enough to enjoy playing for the next couple of years. Rachel liked basketball and seemed to enjoy the work we did together, certainly more than jogging with me.

She had been playing pickup basketball for a couple of years. When she started at age 13, she was playing at the park in McIntosh with me and neighborhood kids and adults. We often had eight to 10 players and played pretty intense games a couple of times a week. At 13, she was already tall, about 5 feet 10 inches, but had not caught up to her height yet and had a hard time with coordination. Initially, she couldn't catch the ball well, passed poorly, and turned the ball over frequently. But the guys all encouraged her and never made her feel left out, even if they didn't pass her the ball much. I always tried to be on her team and get her the ball in a way she could catch and shoot, and she made progress. When we moved to Roanoke in the fall of 2004, she had the chance to play on a homeschool girls' team. It was the first time she played organized basketball and the first time she played with just girls. She didn't start, but she played in most games, had fun, and wanted more. The team had ages up to 18, so at 14, she was one of the youngest.

Rachel is very coachable, always trying to understand and apply what you teach her. In my one-on-one games with her, I was getting a lot of offensive rebounds and second-chance points, so we worked on boxing out. I wanted her to concentrate on keeping me off the offensive boards. During one visit to the park, we worked on that a little, played a one-on-one game, and then asked two guys playing at the other end of the court if they wanted to play a little two-on-two. They agreed and further agreed that I could play on Rachel's team. These were two guys who appeared to be 18 to 20 years old and were fairly short. Rachel and I had the height, but I think the guys figured we would be pretty easy, just an old fart and his young daughter. We beat them 21–8. Next, they asked for a rematch, making some adjustments in the way they played and improving the second time. They went out to an 8–2 lead but then began to miss some outside shots. Rachel and I made a comeback and won the second game 21–18. We thanked one another for the game and went home.

As we walked home, I asked Rachel for her analysis of the game. "I got tired the second game," she said, "and I started missing most of my shots."

"Anything else?" I asked.

"Well, when I got tired, I didn't do as good a job of boxing out, and my guy got some offensive rebounds," she added.

"Anything else?" I asked again.

"No, nothing I can think of."

"Rachel," I exclaimed. "Think about what happened. In the first game, the guy who guarded you was the weaker player. In the second game, they decided to put the stronger player on you. They did that because you dominated them in the first game. You ate their lunch! They couldn't stop the Rachel-scoring-machine. They had to adjust their game plan to account for you. When was the last time that happened?"

"Oh!" She thought about it for a minute, and a gentle smile crept over her face. "That feels pretty good."

It sure did.

LEARNING FROM MISTAKES

For years after I first heard the George Santayana quote—"Those who cannot remember the past are condemned to repeat it"—I thought of it in the context of leaders and their opportunity to learn the macro lessons of history so they could lead their countries more wisely. I still think it is true in that sense, but now I also think of it in the micro sense much more frequently. As I have raised children and mentored a generation of residents, I see that the inability to learn from mistakes is incredibly limiting. As a physician, I hear patients say they don't expect their doctors to be perfect, but they do expect them to acknowledge mistakes, learn from them, and avoid repeating them. Patients will forgive a mistake when the physician takes responsibility for it, apologizes for the inconvenience and damage to the patient, and discloses how this mistake will be taken as the starting point for an improvement in quality.

There is a famous cancer center in Boston where a patient died as a result of a very preventable medication error. The patient's family was given a large settlement, which they turned into a donation to that same center to fund quality improvement efforts. That center went public with its error, made itself accountable for making sure the mistake would never happen again, and, over time, became known for its leadership in patient safety. What would have happened if the hospital had denied the problem, obscured the truth, and tried to cover it up? Its reputation would have been damaged all the more, and even more importantly, it would have missed the opportunity to grow, to improve, and to become a leader. The mistake is not admirable in any sense, but the appropriate response to it is fully admirable. Are there applications for this story in my life? I think so.

For many, the initial response when we are confronted with a mistake we have made is to deny it. Why? As children, we may have learned we would receive correction or discipline when we made a mistake. To avoid an unpleasant correction or discipline, the easiest way is to hope the mistake is not discovered or, when discovered, to deny responsibility or the reality of the error. If denial is successful, the unpleasant consequence is avoided, and the behavior (denial) is rewarded. The short-term reward is more important to the child than the long-term opportunity to develop character and improve a process. Adults usually can see the long-term benefit but may still choose to avoid the short-term unpleasantness. Sometimes our denial behavior has become so ingrained that we don't even recognize we are doing it. For me, I think the larger problem is pride—perhaps the most ubiquitous and difficult of sins. It gets in the way of so much growth, of so much service to others, of peacemaking, of meekness, of gentleness, of a servant relationship to God. Humility, the absence of pride, allows the easy admission of something less than perfection. Humility is not just before God but before people, before our wives, before our children. If my children struggle to demonstrate humility in their lives, is it possible I am not modeling it for them? While it is easy to admit I am not perfect in the abstract, admitting it in a specific circumstance is more challenging.

Rachel played on a homeschool basketball team. The coach, a volunteer who gave extensively of her time, was a great role model and had a servant's heart. She was not a highly experienced coach, though, and didn't know how to coach Rachel's position. I had played that position and knew more than she knew, but I was not the coach. Halfway into the season, Rachel and I had a few practice sessions on weekends, and I worked with her on some of the basics, seeing subsequent improvement during the games. I began to offer encouraging comments from the sidelines, and she responded and played better. (This is still painful to write, although it happened years ago.) Over the course of only a couple of games, my comments from the sidelines got more frequent and more directive. One morning, an email was sent to all us parents, reminding us that there was only one coach, and while we could yell encouragement (good shot!), it was definitely not our role to coach. Our daughters would not be able to be on the team if we did not follow this policy. There could not have been any doubt in the minds of anyone who attended the games who the target of that email was.

I wrote back an email, attacking the public reprimand and pointing out that Rachel had played better. It was about three pages long, beautifully constructed, and logical; it touched on all the important points and even quoted scripture a couple of times. I deleted it almost immediately (thankfully before sending it). I then wrote a less attacking, less extensive one, but it was still skillfully defensive. It, too, went rapidly into the trash file. My third try was this: "I know this was directed at me. I'm sorry. It won't happen again." This one I sent.

I didn't sleep much that night or the following one—or the next one. The games, my behavior, the email, my response, my embarrassment, my shame, the games, my behavior—I reviewed and rehearsed them in my brain over and over. During one of those days, a coworker asked me how it was going, and I told him about what I had done. He looked at me for a minute and then said, "I did the same thing a couple years ago, coaching my son during soccer games. One of the other fathers confronted me. It was embarrassing but not quite as public as what happened to you. It's okay. You are not an evil person." His encouragement meant a lot to me as I was feeling pretty low.

I missed the next couple of Rachel's games due to conflicts or because they were away games. With some considerable trepidation, I then went to one. Either Ben or Dorothy was playing in an early game, with Rachel's game to follow. I went in as unobtrusively as possible and slunk into an obscure seat, but I wasn't able to hide. One of the leaders in the homeschool league was sitting with Rachel's coach, saw me come in, and immediately waved me over to sit with them. They were friendly, warm, accepting, and clearly indicated a complete forgiveness and desire to continue a relationship. It was really only after their response that I could finally get over it. I have come to understand that sleepless nights and mental review are how I deal with very difficult circumstances. The whole process is emotionally painful, draining, and altogether unpleasant. However, it does produce results. Having gone through that, I am extremely unlikely to make *that* mistake again.

Other mistakes are less embarrassing and lead to lesser degrees of sleeplessness. But my brain often nags at me, and in reviewing a situation, I find insight. Fairly recently, we had a team of consultants visit our new and developing medical school to assess our progress, and they set up a mock site visit to prepare us for the real site visit to come. We had prior experience with these consultants, and I really did not like one of them. During our mock site visit, he did some things I found offensive and antagonistic, but rather than shouting at him or going over and punching him in the nose, I got quiet, short, and to the point when responding to him. Although we said nothing of note, it was clear to everyone in the room that he and I were not going to be buddies anytime soon.

A week later during a debriefing session with all our executive team, a couple of pointed suggestions were made to me about how I should continue to smile and be engaged during a site visit, no matter how poorly it might be going. Although I wasn't particularly singled out for the suggestions—each person had something different to work on—that night I woke up out of a sound sleep at 12:30 a.m. and thought about the mock visit and the debriefing. After stewing about it for a while, I eventually put it in this context. Not punching him in the nose was good; it got me a C grade rather than an F. Now let's talk about how I could get an A and be focused on that instead of his offensive behavior. When the time came for the real site visit, things were fine. My debrief was this: You were relaxed, and your body language showed you were confident, open, and glad to be there. Good job. An A.

A few years ago, I interviewed 72 seniors in medical school for 12 positions in a residency program I ran. They were the cream of the crop from medical school, almost all in the top of their class, all going into highly competitive residencies. I asked each of them, "Have you ever failed at anything?"

Only about 10 percent responded, "Sure, I've failed at lots of things, some of them pretty important." The rest struggled, unsure of how to answer, unsure of what I was getting at, clearly never having considered this question before. I can tell you I am much more comfortable choosing someone who understands that failure is part of life and who has already developed a correct response. I sometimes share with them that I have learned much more from my failures than my successes. I enjoy success, but it doesn't wake me up in the middle of the night. Success doesn't prompt much insight in me, and it doesn't modify my behavior.

As a residency director, I discussed incidents that came to my attention with residents. These were often complaints about something the resident had done, usually focused on their professionalism, and came from patients, peers, or nurses. As I went over the complaint, the residents were usually defensive. They had another viewpoint of the incident, they thought most of the blame for the incident belonged elsewhere, and they thought their actions had been misunderstood. They responded exactly as I had responded (see above). I learned I had to have a brief discussion initially and then schedule another meeting in a couple of days. I asked them to consider that if only 10 percent of the problem was theirs, they should take ownership of that part and think about how they might have acted differently. Usually, in a couple of days we could have a discussion that led to improvement.

I also learned that I needed to have a discussion with them earlier in their training. I would meet with the new residents and ask them to raise their hands if they were perfect. None did. I asked them to raise a hand if they knew everything they needed to know about being a pediatrician. None did. I asked them if they thought I had a role in helping them become good doctors. Everyone raised a hand. "Good," I said. "We have established that you will likely make mistakes and that I have a role in teaching you how to avoid doing the same thing in the future. When we identify such an occasion, we understand that my correction is part of the training program, that I won't think less of you, that you won't regard the correction as character assassination, and that we will both move on without damage to our relationship. I will continue to think just as highly of you as I do right now." One resident told me a year later that this discussion really took the stress off her as she worried much less about the need to be perfect. My discussions with them when an incident required my intervention became much easier and more productive.

I never had this discussion with my children; I hadn't learned enough to do so. But I have had it with my grandchildren on occasion, and perhaps it helped them be more receptive to a learning opportunity.

We live in a society that puts much value on self-esteem and one that wants to emphasize the positive and not focus on the negative. Parents and teachers are told to be supportive, encouraging, and positive, and pointing out failures is considered less than ideal because it damages the all-important self-esteem. We have an educational system that is worse and worse, families that are failing, and an increasingly dysfunctional society. The reason is not simply a wrong focus on self-esteem, though that is certainly part of it. If God values humility so much, why would we think that taking it out of our daily lives would be good? (Watch professional basketball or football players woof and trash talk one another, and see if you can point out to me their meekness and humility. This behavior is now seen at all levels of competition.) As parents, we have to transmit a message to our children that we love them despite their failures, that we value them always, and that part of our love and commitment to them is to help them improve. That includes, necessarily, an attention to failure.

MASCULINITY

We were up at Maple Ridge, and Dorothy called me to ask to use my car. She needed to drive to North Carolina to meet her mother-in-law and pick up her children after a visit to Florida, a change from the original plan. I was sympathetic, acknowledged that changes in plans were sometimes challenging, and said sure, she could use my car. As we said goodbye, I heard a catch in her voice, as though she were fighting back tears. A few minutes later, I commented to Linda, "Dorothy sounded like she was crying. I'm not sure why, but maybe you should call her and make sure she is okay."

She did and then reported, "She is fine. She just said that you were so understanding and sympathetic that it got to her. She was a little surprised that it made her cry, but she is okay."

I sometimes comment that I am a pale shadow of the man I once was. I now watch and enjoy the Hallmark Channel, am perfectly happy to miss a football game, and am lots more willing to not be in control of everything around me. I am easier to get along with and have developed a surprising reputation for being empathetic and gentle. I think my testosterone levels are low. My son Chris just shakes his head about this sad state of affairs. My daughters wonder why it took so long for me to mature.

After my knee replacement and subsequent herniated disc repair, I was in need of some serious rehab. I can't run anymore but can walk vigorously, which is good aerobic exercise, low impact, and something I can do without having to go to the gym. I usually take Lucy (our Labradoodle) with me. Lucy is very cute with tight black curls, very friendly, and loves to walk. When she comes back from a grooming, she usually has cloth flowers on her head, just above her ears. Did I mention she is very cute? For our walks, I dress in gym shorts and a T-shirt with the sleeves cut off because I like the freedom and have impressive arms. One day we walked up a hill, and I was puffing a little as we passed a man of mature age doing something with his truck. Just past him, the road ended, so we circled back and passed him again. I heard him say something but didn't quite catch it. "I'm sorry, I missed that. Were you saying something to me?"

"Yeah. Do you do that to your dog?"

"You mean the flowers on her head?"

"Yeah."

"She comes back from the groomers like that. I think they're cute."

"Yeah, I guess so." End of conversation.

As I continued my walk, I began to consider the implications of this brief communication and developed a deeper understanding of what had just happened. I had passed a man working on his *truck*. Trucks are manly, and a man who has one is making a statement about his masculinity. If it is a four-wheel drive, has a big engine, and can jerk out tree stumps, it *must* belong to a very manly man. Dogs for such a man are likely to be pit bulls, Rottweilers, or German shepherds. Such a man would certainly not decorate his Labradoodle, if he were unfortunate enough to own one, with flowers in her hair. This man had been confused by the conflicting image of me (bald, beard, exercising, muscles, man) and dog (cute, gentle, flowers in her hair) and had tried to reconcile them. I could have helped by saying, "My pit bull is at the vet getting stitches from his last dog fight, and I have to walk this ridiculous dog that belongs to my teenage daughter." I wasn't quick enough to do so, however, and left him with some serious questions about my masculinity.

When I got home, I talked to Linda about this, thinking she wouldn't like to be married to a man with masculinity issues. She was surprisingly unconcerned. I pointed out that I was driving a

Toyota Camry Hybrid, and she was driving an all-wheel drive SUV. Perhaps we should trade. She declined. I pushed a little harder. She was unyielding. I'm stuck with the hybrid. I do own a big four-wheel drive, three-quarter-ton truck with a diesel engine, but it gets such bad mileage I don't drive it unless I have to. But the next time I drive it, I'm going to take a detour up that hill and hope that guy recognizes me.

I also talked to my doctor. In addition to becoming gentle and understanding, I had gained some weight and suspected my basal metabolic rate was slowing down. He suggested weight training, l-arginine, and measuring my testosterone level. Turns out that aerobic exercise (handball, jogging, walking) increases your metabolic rate (and therefore burns calories) for a couple of hours, but weight training increases the metabolic rate for 24 hours. L-arginine aids secretion of a growth hormone, which has beneficial effects on metabolism as well. I wasn't excited about testosterone supplements, but he thought they would be good if my levels were excessively low. I told Linda about the plan.

"Ooooh, I need to talk to your doctor."

"Why?"

"I don't want you to go back to the way you used to be. I like the new you."

So much for thinking she wouldn't want to be married to a man with masculinity issues.

ANGER, SIN, OR USEFUL TOOL?

If you had asked me if anger was a significant problem for me, I would have been surprised at the question, wondered why you asked it, and denied it.

I would have acknowledged that I love competitive sports and have engaged in lots of them. It is also true that my competitive spirit sometimes led to violent confrontation that went beyond friendly competition, but not all that often. (One time when playing intramural football, I got into a fight with someone on the other team. I tried to shake his hand after the game, and he told me he should have stayed away from me because I had picked a fight with him last year, too.)

In Vietnam, during a combat operation, one of my platoon members got his leg blown off when he walked into a field of booby traps. None of the soldiers near him would go to his aid, fearing the minefield would get them, too. I became so angry at their inaction that I walked into the danger zone, picked him up, and carried him out of the area. While the outcome was fine for the soldier and I got a medal for the action, the motive would have been far better if it had been motivated by self-sacrifice for the good of another rather than an angry desire to show up the others who were more self-protective. My anger caused me to do something foolish, and the good could have been accomplished in a better way.

Before I go further, let me say that anger, as used in this essay, is more than emotion—it is tied to how that emotion is expressed.

In all that follows, anger led to behavior that was combative, confrontational, and aggressive in my behavior or voice. It was not constructive or protective.

Two events caused me to reconsider whether I had an anger problem. One day, my grown son called me to ask for forgiveness for bitterness he had carried for years. He told me that when I had lost my temper, it caused him to be frightened of me and made living with me difficult and almost unbearable. He had considered running away. He acknowledged that my anger was often not directed toward him but affected him deeply. I was surprised. I did not think I got angry very often and certainly didn't know it had that effect on him. I called my two oldest sons and asked them. Neither harbored bitterness and did not need me to ask for their forgiveness. (They are wonderful men but not as overwhelmingly gentle and empathetic as their brother.) I then remembered a time when I became angry with my youngest son. Shortly after that event, when I had calmed down, he told me it really bothered him when I lost my temper. I think I told him at the time that he wouldn't be subject to that anger if he behaved better.

Think about that brief conversation—he approached me without being difficult, without anger, but with an observation that my behavior had a negative effect on him. He did not deny that he had done something to trigger it, and he did not justify himself. He simply told me that my actions negatively affected our relationship. His approach to me was perfectly reasonable. And my response? I did not acknowledge any wrong action. I essentially excused my behavior by linking it to his behavior. I had an opportunity to self-reflect and learn something from my son, yet I rejected the opportunity. It was nearly a decade ago, and I am just now coming to a place of acceptance and growth.

I still feel that my episodes of anger were relatively rare. Is that an excuse for not dealing with the problem? Christ said that if you become angry with someone (and call them a fool), it is the equivalent of murder. If I murder only occasionally, is that acceptable? If I murder once, can I justify it by saying, "Well, I'm not a serial killer." So if I acknowledge that occasionally I get angry and behave poorly, then I have to acknowledge I have an anger issue.

This thought process, this writing, this acceptance is *very* hard for me. It is painful. It makes me feel exposed and raw in a way different from the vulnerability in most of my other essays. I think I am slowly understanding why, but I am not sure my understanding is complete. For one thing, I think this issue has hurt the people I love the most—my wife and children. The understanding that I would do something over and over again that hurt them, that damaged our relationship, and that perhaps restricted my ability to protect and minister to them causes me pain. The undeniable truth that I was given many opportunities to accept the failure and work to correct it but repeatedly rejected that opportunity makes it worse. I think I now understand that I used that anger to control others. I wanted them to fear my anger more than they wanted to do the forbidden thing and thus decide not to do it. Perhaps it was my insecurity that led to the thought that fear would control them, but loving me and wanting my approval would not.

Children have a need for love and discipline. These are not mutually exclusive; they can be administered simultaneously. Discipline may be very unpleasant, but the one doing the discipline can still love deeply and be loved. Anger drives people away. Anger causes the object of that anger to doubt the love. Anger is selfish, making things better only for the one practicing it. Angry outbursts are normal in childhood development but should go away as children mature. Anger issues that persist into adulthood are evidence of a failure to mature. They are not healthy and not appropriate.

I am very aware that children and adults respond much more to praise than criticism. Praise and acknowledgment of excellence are much better motivators in the workplace and at home than criticism and punishment. In fact, as I grew as a father, I used them and have seen their superior efficacy. As I gained experience as a father, I used positive reinforcement more often and discipline less often. My anger came out less often but remained an issue, and I suspect my children and wife will have differing thoughts about the magnitude of the problem. My relationship with them at this time is loving and supportive. I feel they generally regard me as having been a good father. I am grateful that they see more good than bad and that they have continued to respect me despite my faults. But I now regret the anger and clearly see it as sin, never a useful tool.

My children have reviewed these essays. Two of my sons sent me long replies. Clearly they have thought about anger in their own lives and how it is manifested and affects their children. One acknowledged that he has used anger as a controlling force in his own family. My essay came at a time when he was already confronting this in his life. His response was this: "Yeah, Dad, I have this problem, too, and this is how I am thinking about it." The other son initially said he had recognized that I had anger issues during his childhood and had tried to avoid them as a parent. A week later, he wrote again, this time reflecting that perhaps his issues were more subtle but were there nonetheless. I deeply appreciate their self-reflection. I am deeply thankful that my children love me despite my sinfulness.

MUSIC

"Jim, would you consider being in a musical?" my voice teacher asked. "It is *Take Me Along,* and we need men who can sing and dance. You would be perfect since you dance as well." There was no need to audition; they were desperate for warm bodies for the chorus line.

I was enrolled at the University of South Florida in Tampa. I had been discharged from the army that spring and had taught swimming lessons over the summer, and now at USF, I was a pre-med chemistry major. Since I had done almost all science and math classes in the two years of college before going into the army, I had only chemistry left to take but needed general credits. I took visual arts, voice lessons, modern dance, anthropology, social sciences—anything that looked interesting. I had always been interested in theater, singing, and dance, and I enjoyed performing. I looked forward to being in the musical, one of the big productions for the theater department that semester.

In that production, I also met Linda. She was the rehearsal pianist, which was part of the requirement for her work-study program as a piano major. Although we did not start dating until I met her again at the beach that summer, it was fitting that we should meet at something that involved music since music has been part of our relationship ever since. When our family grew, we began singing a couple of hymns in the mornings before our family devotions, and we sang to the children as part of their bedtime routine. Chris could recognizably sing a couple of songs before he was a year old and before he could say anything beyond "mama." Shockingly, Timo couldn't carry a tune until he was about three. I would have wondered if the nurses had switched babies in the nursery if he hadn't been the identical image of Linda. He had to be ours.

In Vermont, we began to sing as a family. The first song we worked on was something about the good seed God gave us to scatter on the ground. We taught Scott and Chris their parts through endless repetition, and then we sang a four-part harmony in church. Chris still groans at the thought of the "Goodsie, Goodsie" song. We moved a lot, but when we were in a church with a choir, the children were expected (when old enough) to sing with the adult choir and certainly with the children's choir when they had the opportunity.

When we lived in McIntosh, Florida, Linda became the choir director, ordering music and having access to all the music in the library. We all had favorites, and when our extended family came for a visit, we often sat around and read parts from hymnals or went to the church and brought home anthems to read through. Everyone liked to sing, and we didn't care that it wasn't always very musical. We laughed at our mistakes and had a great time. Whatever else we might be doing, singing time caused everyone to gather.

"Why don't we get serious about this?" I asked.

Linda and her mother thought that was a great idea, and so did everyone else. The kids seemed excited, and the Family Chorale was born. Over the next two years, we bought music, met for practice, and sang as a family in a couple of venues. Mostly, the group was family, although we had at least one extra family member. We joined with our churches for one cantata and with the community for a Christmas program. We sang at the 1890's Festival in McIntosh, at Silver Springs for a Christmas concert, at church, and at Miracle Mountain Ranch in northern Pennsylvania. Scott, Chris, and Gary (Linda's brother) had to travel to get to practice, but they made the effort. This period culminated in the recording of *Beginnings*, the CD of our favorite songs.

The CD could have been called *Finishings* as well. After that effort, the impetus and time for the Family Chorale seemed to be over. I think most of the family (though maybe not some of the youngest children) have really good memories of the time we spent together. We met for a common purpose, everyone had an important part, and we made something that could not have been made without everyone's input. We had fellowship, and we enjoyed the time together. The commitment in time and distance eventually became a burden, however, so that chapter came to an end.

Music in one form or another has continued to be a major part of our lives. In recent years, Linda and I have become heavily involved in barbershop-style singing. For a time, Ben and I sang in a barbershop quartet named Ben and the Boyz. We practiced intently, sang in contests, and once won an award as the best novice quartet. More recently, Linda and I have sung in a mixed quartet named Fine Whine. We enjoy the technical aspects of this style of singing and have become pretty involved in it. The thread through all these different experiences is the shared passion, the common experience, and the love of doing something meaningful with the people we love.

All the children continue to have a love for music and still enjoy singing together. Most play instruments, and most are involved in a worship team at church. Linda really gets the credit for this—she is a wonderful musician with a great ear and a highly tuned desire to praise God with her talent, and fortunately the children have benefited from her influence. Timo was once asked if everyone in the family was musically gifted. He thought carefully for a moment and responded, "No, not really. All my dad can do is sing." He is correct, but I really like doing that, especially along with my gifted family.

SONG LYRICS

I have no talent in painting or drawing, but I enjoy painting with words. In some sense, poetry is more artistic than standard composition, allowing me to put away the rules of grammar and punctuation. The author is free to use words and rhythm to paint a picture using innuendos and hints. I like the challenge of rhythm and rhyme and incorporate these elements in most of my poetry, which makes it, I think, old-fashioned. For lyrics, this works well. The varieties of music I enjoy have structure and rhythm and usually have lyrics that rhyme. Because I have no gift for musical composition, most of the lyrics I have written have been set to existing music.

The final six years of my career as a physician were spent in the well newborn nursery, taking care of newborns in the first days after their birth. I taught family practice and pediatric residents how to do newborn medicine, and they spent four weeks with me. I also taught medical students and PA (physician assistant) students, who spent a week with me. Circumcisions were part of the job and took up a significant part of the day. To add a little variety, I came up with some circumcision songs. The first was to the tune of "The Lion Sleeps Tonight" and contained a chorus of "a-weeney-whack, a-weeney whack." Students enjoyed the song, and new students on the rotation would ask for it if a few days went by and I had not yet sung it. In a quest for variety, I then created a blues song titled "I've Got the Bad Circumcision Blues" and a parody of the "Cups" song from *Pitch Perfect*.

One student told Linda, "Your husband is a legend. Everybody knows about his circumcision songs." It would have been nice to be a legend for teaching excellence, but I guess I shouldn't be too choosey.

My most successful attempt to write lyrics came about through a chance exposure. Linda and I were at a party hosted by Merrill Lynch. The guests were invited to take a seat in a theater and enjoy entertainment by David Stewart Wiley (DSW), the conductor of the Roanoke Symphony, arranger, composer, and wonderful pianist. He spoke, played, and accompanied a soprano. It was a wonderful 30 minutes listening to very accomplished musicians. One piece he played was "Concentric Circles," a piano piece he had composed for a movie called *Lake Effects* shot at Smith Mountain Lake. The score of the movie included the piece as played by the Roanoke Symphony, but we just heard the piano solo version. I was quite impressed by the music. It was joyful, interesting, soaring, and beautiful, and lasted about three to four minutes. I wondered if there were words. Later in the evening, as we were standing around chatting, DSW made his way around to the guests, greeting, chatting, and accepting his just accolades. He briefly joined our little group, and there were pleasantries. Before he left, I asked, "I really enjoyed 'Concentric Circles'; are there lyrics?" There were not. "Well, could I write some?" He looked a little taken aback but said, "Well, sure. I'll send you the music." I never got any music and could not find a written score from any music source. I let it drop.

In October 2016, the Barbershop Harmony Society sent out a request for proposals for grants to support a cappella singing. I decided to try to organize an a cappella festival with the many vocal groups in the area. While most of them used accompanied singing, I guessed they would all have some a cappella music in their repertoire. I also figured that if the most renowned musician in the area bought into the idea, it would open doors otherwise closed to me. I had a good friend who was a friend of David Stewart Wiley. My friend arranged a lunch meeting with the three of us, I pitched the idea, and DSW agreed to help. During that discussion, I brought up the possibility of doing the premiere performance of a song written for the festival and suggested "Concentric Circles." I have no idea if DSW even remembered my original offer to write lyrics, but he said, "Sure, I'll send you the music." Within a day, I had his handwritten piano score, digital recordings of the piano version, and the symphony version. I went to work.

I needed a theme. I looked first at the movie, but the movie is about resolving a conflict, and to me, the music's overwhelming feel was one of joy and celebration. A friend of mine loves "Lullabye," a Billy Joel composition that touches his soul and reminds him of the love he has for his daughter. I wanted to do something like that, something that resonated with my deepest feelings about being a parent. I ran that by DSW, who was okay with it. (An aside about DSW. He is a busy man with no time to beat around the bush. If you work with him on a project, you get his thoughts and feelings without much filtering. If he doesn't like it, he will say so. He also responds very quickly. When he sees an email, he deals with it right then. Since that is pretty much my style, I respect and enjoy that kind of relationship.)

I listened to the music, looking for the underlying structure. Songs, music, and lyrics are often composed together and have a structure made to fit the needs of each. Songs usually have an emotional climax, either at the end or repetitively in the chorus. Often, it is the lyrics that are the focus, and the melody supports the lyrics. "Concentric Circles" was written by an accomplished composer who wanted to create something complex, written without consideration of lyrics, and something challenging enough to be interesting to people knowledgeable about music. The music had two areas of emotional climax, neither of which was in the usual place for a song. It had rhythmic complexity. The points of musical emphasis varied in different measures. It certainly had structure, but it was very different than anything I had previously done. I graphed out the structure I would need to match. It took days.

When I started writing lyrics, it went pretty well for the first two verses, but then I got stuck. I spent hours trying one idea and then another. I didn't like any of them. I tried something else and thought it was a little better. Linda didn't like it, and really, I didn't, either. She made a suggestion that I also didn't like. A couple of weeks went on. I should have been working on the grant application but couldn't—I was focused on the lyrics. On a Sunday when I had nothing else scheduled, I stayed home from church (I had an excuse since I was on call and had gone into the hospital that morning) and tried again. This time, the muse struck, and I got something. It wasn't perfect, but it wasn't too bad. I worked on it until I liked it, but one section was still incomplete. A couple of days and many hours later, waking up in the middle of the night with the music and lyrics chasing each other around in my brain, I finally had something. Linda liked it, too, but suggested I make some minor changes in the music to make it more singable. I was not about to make any changes to DSW's music. "He can make those changes; I'm not going to." Linda used her music composition software to write out the melody with the words under the appropriate notes. (I had tried to do it freehand and had given up in frustration.) We edited it, made it look good, and saved it as an attachment. I got up the next morning and composed an email to DSW with the attachment and then poised my finger over the send button. And I stopped.

Who am I to write lyrics for a DSW composition? This man is an expert in his area, and I am a rank novice. I may be an expert in medicine but certainly not music. What was I thinking? What if he thinks this is trash? What if he thinks I am an idiot just wasting his time? All this went on in my head. I hesitantly pushed the send button and was immediately anxious, awaiting his response. Linda was amused. "Forty-five years of marriage and this is the first time I've seen you so intimidated." She was right; I was intimidated. Fortunately, DSW was complimentary, we worked through some edits, and it was finished.

I didn't know what would happen to the music and lyrics. I hoped I would hear it someday but wasn't at all sure that would happen. But even if I never heard it, the experience is one I treasure. I am very grateful to DSW for allowing me to stretch to do this.

Without the music, it is probably difficult to see why this was so hard for me, but I offer the lyrics alone as poetry about what it means to be a parent. One point I wanted to make was that children know their parents love them, but they never really understand the extent of that love until they have their own child. Another point is that children do not owe anything to their parents for all the sacrificial love they have been given, except to give that same kind of love to their children. (This reminds me of the message from Christ to love others as God has loved us.)

I remember when I held you
Sleeping in my arms, secure
My heart was filled with loving you, my child
Like I'd never loved before

I remember when you first walked
Arms held high to reach your goal
Taking first a tiny step and then you ran
Calling "Catch me if you can"

When you wanted independence
When you wanted to explore
I just had to let you learn to fly
I just had to let you soar

And you flew far and wide
To the sky, to the moon, to the stars
And yet you stayed by my side
Your success somehow became ours

Now you're holding your child
And your heart opens wide
As you look at their face
I see you comprehend,
All my love, paying now its dividend
Concentric Circles of love
Touching all our lives

The grant didn't get funded, just in case you wondered.

A couple of years later, I attended the premiere performance of "Concentric Circles," the song. It was performed by the Roanoke Valley Children's Chorus with David Stewart Wiley accompanying them on the piano. In his introduction of the song, David had me stand up and then spoke very graciously about the lyrics and how they had come to be. The song (music and lyrics) were well received, and it was certainly a wonderful conclusion to this creative journey and a kind of bucket list moment.

GETTING FEEBLE

When Ben and I got involved in barbershop singing, and particularly after we formed Ben and the Boyz, we had lots of opportunities to sing in retirement communities and nursing homes. The quality of life in these communities is quite varied but pretty dismal in some of them. In nursing homes in particular, the residents have little residual function, either physical or mental, and need a lot of help with simple tasks of daily living. I made no secret of the fact that I hated the thought of being so dependent on others and hated the thought of my children and their families having to deal with me in that state.

All the top choices on my list of good ways to die were sudden and did not deal with long-term decline. As I write this, I am 72 and still capable of independent living, but the signs of deterioration in my physical abilities are pretty obvious. I guess I spoke of my distaste of others having to take care of me, and my daughter-in-law Kara wanted to give me a different perspective. She remembered a children's story from her youth, searched it out, purchased the book online, and happily gave it to me for Christmas, explaining that the book illustrated the joy of caring for someone who once cared for you. The story is quite sweet. A retired gentleman takes a neighbor's daughter for walks and along the way protects her from any harm. He very much enjoys their time together, and it is clear he is a loving and wonderful companion for her. Then, tragically, his health declines, and he is no longer capable of caring for her. She is somewhat older now and shows up at his house to take him outside in his wheelchair for a walk. She enjoys his company and shows herself to be a loving and protecting companion. They have reversed roles.

It seemed to me that Kara was far too excited about this future for our relationship. I hated the thought, while she seemed happy at the prospect. I appreciated her love; I just didn't like the idea.

Recently, the pastor of our church was discussing the birth of Christ and presented some truth in a way I had not previously considered. The first chapter of John makes it clear that since the beginning of time, Christ has been part of the triune God—the creator of the universe, the same God who challenged Job by asking him if he could direct the leviathan of the deep or cause a storm. God never explained himself to Job; He simply said that Job had no right to question Him. God describes Himself as all-powerful, as a jealous God, as wise. There is nothing weak, nothing dependent, and nothing feeble about God. But then He became an infant, totally dependent, completely weak, requiring help with His most basic needs. God, for my sake, became the kind of person I have hated becoming. Ouch! I have had to reconsider my thoughts and realize that refusing to become what Christ became is a manifestation of great pride. I have been too proud to accept the possibility of becoming Christ-like in this particular regard. If it did happen, would I be bitter and unaccepting, making it even more difficult for those caring for me? Or would I accept the path God has for me, praise and worship Him, and "count it all joy" (James 1:2). I hope the latter. My children are encouraged to read this to me if I am grumpy about my state.

When I showed this to Kara, she assured me she was not excited at the prospect of my decline, just willing to see it in a positive light. I still prefer the sudden options on my list.

A MISUNDERSTANDING

I got a text from Dorothy while I was out shopping. "Are you at Walmart?" I was. She called and asked, "Please pick up a box of Pampers, size four, Cruisers, for Julianna." I went to the grocery section and found paper towels, napkins, and toilet paper, but no diapers. I wandered around the kids' clothes section; no diapers. After a while, I decided I needed help and approached a young man who was stocking the shelves. "Where are disposable diapers?" I inquired.

"I'll show you," he said and led the way to the pharmacy section, stopping at the beginning of a short aisle. "The disposable diapers are just beyond the dental supplies." I went down the aisle and found Depends, diapers for leaky adults of a certain age.

Now, I know I'm old and look it. I've had a tough life and a few knocks. I've had cancer, knee and shoulder replacement, and two episodes of back surgery. I'm bald and wrinkled, sometimes cannot remember why I went upstairs, and show up at events at the wrong time—but I don't leak.

I went back to find the Walmart guy and looked until I found the same one. It might not make any difference to him, but I wanted to clear up any misunderstanding he had. "I need baby diapers, not adult ones."

"Oh, they are just past pet supplies." That makes sense—pets, kids, they're a lot alike. I found the Pampers. Cruisers, size four. They work fine on Julianna. I still don't need them.

KRISTIN'S POEM

Kristin gave me this on my 61st birthday. The references to guidance, eggs, and jogging are all explained, to some extent, in these *Essays on Fatherhood*. Kristin beautifully put into words something very important. Although fathers often fail, children can learn the lessons and get past the imperfections of their fathers. That perspective is a wonderful gift from God.

Dear Daddy

As a baby I listened to your voice
Surrounded by siblings not making a noise
We piled on the couch, raptured by the story
Of an elephant or mouse in their moment of glory

Even though it's not often been said
Sitting with you before going to bed
Was a moment of bonding that was yours and mine
Something I'll treasure for all of time

As a child I listened to your voice
"Eat your eggs!" I did not have a choice
In spite of my age, you saw cause for concern
Obedience was a lesson I needed to learn

Even though it's not often been said

You've taught me submitting's not something to dread
I'm grateful for the patience you've shown to me
As I learn to become what God wants me to be

As a teen I listened to your voice
"Running is reason enough to rejoice!"
There were many times that it caused us to fight
But I've found that, as usual, you were right

Even though it's not often been said
Running with you is a way I've been led
To trust what you ask when I don't understand
How God fits what you ask of me into His plan

As I look through my years, the choices I've made
Have often left my life tangled and frayed
But you've always held your arms open wide
When I've finally come, repentant, to your side
The love for me in your heart never changing
As you help me to keep the same mistakes from making

I know you are human and therefore can sin
But your love for me I've never needed to win
I'm grateful that God has allowed you to be
The example of His unending love for me
And all these lessons learned that are yours and mine
Are something I'll treasure for all of time!

I love you very much!
Kristin

ABOUT THE AUTHOR

James Sherman, a retired pediatric pulmonologist, is the father of eight children. He and Linda, his wife of 47 years, live in a house that he and his family built in rural southwest Virginia. They homeschooled all their children and are now grandparents to 19 grandchildren. Jim began to write essays about their family journey years ago to preserve important details for future generations. Those essays led to this book. In many ways, these essays are the testimony of the work of Christ in Jim's life.

CPSIA information can be obtained
at www.ICGtesting.com
Printed in the USA
LVHW050755290920
667371LV00015B/459

9 781735 221724